EXPLORING THE SCIENCE OF SOUNDS

100 Musical Activities For Young Children

by Abigail Flesch Connors

Gryphon House

www.gryphonhouse.com

COPYRIGHT

Bulk Purchase

Gryphon House books are available for special premiums and sales promotions as well as for fund-raising use. Special editions or book excerpts also can be created to specifications. For details, call 800.638.0928.

Disclaimer

Gryphon House, Inc., cannot be held responsible for damage, mishap, or injury incurred during the use of or because of activities in this book. Appropriate and reasonable caution and adult supervision of children involved in activities and corresponding to the age and capability of each child involved are recommended at all times. Do not leave children unattended at any time. Observe safety and caution at all times.

Library of Congress Cataloging-in-Publication Data

Names: Connors, Abigail Flesch, 1957- author.
Title: Exploring the science of sounds : 100 musical activities for young
    children / by Abigail Flesch Connors.
Description: Lewisville, NC : Gryphon House, Inc., [2017] | Includes
    bibliographical references and index. |
Identifiers: LCCN 2017018599 (print) | LCCN 2017023214 (ebook) | ISBN
    9780876597323 () | ISBN 9780876597316 (pbk.)
Subjects: LCSH: Sound--Juvenile literature. | Music--Acoustics and
    physics--Juvenile literature.
Classification: LCC QC225.5 (ebook) | LCC QC225.5 .C65 2017 (print) | DDC
    534.078--dc23
LC record available at https://lccn.loc.gov/2017018599

DEDICATION

To Shannon, with love and gratitude

TABLE OF CONTENTS

Music is a magical thing. It helps us celebrate our joys and ease our sorrows. It excites us, calms us, and enchants us with its mysterious power.

Music is also science.

I first learned this from my wisest teachers—the young children in my music-enrichment classes.

For instance, in one recent class, I was teaching a group of four-year-olds how to tap and scrape rhythm sticks as a recording of instrumental music played in the background. The children happily tapped and scraped to the beat of the music, but they also asked:

"Why do some of the sticks have bumps and some don't?"

"Why are some sticks red and some sticks blue?"

"Why is it louder when I play like this"—holding the sticks flat on the floor—"instead of like this?" (holding them in the air).

"What would happen if I hit the sticks on the floor as hard as I can? Would they break?" This particular question wasn't asked aloud. The child performed this experiment on her own. Fortunately, rhythm sticks are quite sturdy!

So, why were the children asking all these seemingly irrelevant questions? When I was younger, I assumed it was because young children had short attention spans. Years of experience and of exploring what scientists know about how young children learn have changed my opinion. Questions like these aren't irrelevant—they're scientific!

Spoiler alert!

Music activities almost always bring out children's scientific curiosity. Unfortunately, we rarely take advantage of this opportunity to help them develop scientific thinking. Let's go back to one of these questions. A child asked, "Why do some of the sticks have bumps and some don't?"

What if I simply told her, "We need the bumpy sticks to make the scraping sound. If we had only smooth sticks, we couldn't make that sound." Okay. That's a true and fairly age-appropriate response. But what just happened?

1. I "taught" the child a "fact" (that she'll probably forget by tomorrow, anyway).
2. I encouraged her (and the rest of the class) in the common belief among young children that grown-ups know everything.
3. Most troubling, this girl was exhibiting scientific curiosity and I shut it down. Just stopped it in its tracks.

Why bother thinking, observing, listening, and experimenting, if a quick and easy answer is as close as the nearest adult? Giving a child the answer to a question of that nature is like giving away the ending to a book before someone's finished reading it. Have you ever had someone spoil the ending of a book or movie for you? Frustrating, isn't it? It diminishes the exciting experience of wondering what will happen. When we tell children the answer, we're spoiling the ending of the scientific story.

We're keeping them from making their own discoveries, which is an innately satisfying and rewarding experience. We're depriving them of what the physicist Richard Feynman called "the pleasure of finding things out." And it's that pleasure, that excitement, that reinforces children's scientific curiosity.

Young children don't really have short attention spans. They're constantly paying attention to everything in their environment. Their brains are processing vast amounts of information, driven by an urgent need to make meaningful connections, to make sense of their environment—of objects, people, sights and sounds, and of their own bodies and identities. What's more, as Alison Gopnik, Andrew N. Meltzoff, and Patricia K. Kuhl describe in their book *The Scientist in the Crib*, children are constantly revising their theories of how things work as they perceive new information. As a matter of fact, young children do think a lot like scientists, and meaningful science activities in early childhood build the foundation for future science learning.

My students' curious questions were examples of valid and very pertinent scientific inquiry. But I didn't realize that when I was starting out as a music teacher. Back then, not out of an intention to "teach science" but just to be a responsive teacher, I began to follow up on the children's not-on-the-lesson-plan questions. For example, if a child asked what was inside the shakers we were playing, I'd ask the class what they thought was inside. Some would say, "rocks," or "little balls," or something similar. If someone suggested an answer that didn't seem to make sense, such as "an animal," I'd gently challenge their thinking. "Hmm. I'm wondering if an animal could live inside a shaker." Voices would immediately ring out, "No! Animals need food." "They need air to breathe." Before you knew it, the class would be having a wonderful discussion, sharing thoughts and using what they already knew to evaluate ideas. We would come to a consensus that the shakers most likely contained many small, hard objects. (I've never deliberately broken open a shaker in the name of research. But I often share with children a story about the time a shaker accidentally broke during a music class—countless tiny plastic beads flew everywhere!)

These informal discussions inspired me to create activities, such as "Mystery Music Can," in which children take turns shaking a coffee can and guessing what's inside it. I started to collect all kinds of unusual instruments, as well as nontraditional sound makers, such as foam egg cartons and old baskets, which, when scraped with a stick, sounded like a guiro. We'd improvise with ways to play them, think about and discuss how we could change their sounds, and try different ideas to see if they'd work the way we thought they would. For instance, we found that hitting a little glockenspiel with a plastic dinosaur did not make it louder. (Some children always want to make things louder.) Glockenspiels are often confused with xylophones. Technically, though, the instruments with metal bars are glockenspiels. Xylophones have wooden bars.

After a few years, I put my sound-exploration activities together and wrote articles about them for parents and teachers. At professional-development conferences, I presented workshops where early childhood teachers could learn and try out these activities. It was lots of fun, but I was surprised one day when a workshop participant referred to my "science activities." What? No, this is music. I'm not a science person. But when I thought about it, in these sound-exploration activities, the children were observing, listening, asking questions, making predictions, testing ideas, and interpreting results. They were thinking like scientists!

With my amazing students, I tried out more activities exploring the science of music. We learned more about the sound quality (timbre) of various instruments and other objects. We also delved into other elements of music, including tempo and pitch. And we went further, trying to find answers to questions, such as "What is music, anyway?" and "Is there any way we could see music?" The children were fascinated by the process, as well as the content, of what we were learning, and they could be counted on to ask questions I'd never even thought of!

Always curious, I read many books and journal articles about early childhood science education. I found studies showing that many teachers of young children didn't provide enough experiences to foster science skills and build conceptual understanding. Yet, preschoolers are ready and eager to explore science. There was clearly a need for more everyday science activities, not just once-in-a-while special projects.

I wrote this book to address the need for not only more science content but also for more scientific thinking in preschool. First, young children need to be actively observing, listening, questioning, predicting, comparing, and contrasting—and talking about all these processes—to develop their reasoning skills and to preserve their natural curiosity.

Second, it is essential for children to be able to place the science content we teach them in a broader conceptual context. For this, I found the idea of crosscutting concepts, described on the website of the National Science Teachers Association (NSTA), very useful. (See http://ngss.nsta.org/ CrosscuttingConceptsFull.aspx.) Crosscutting concepts can be thought of as the "big ideas" of science. As the NSTA states, "they have application across all domains of science . . . [and] include patterns; cause and effect; scale, proportion and quantity; systems and system models; energy and matter; structure and function; and stability and change." The NSTA stresses that "these concepts need to be made explicit for students." For example, children may find it interesting that the smaller bars on a glockenspiel make higher sounds than the longer bars. This could be just a "Wow, that's cool!" moment, quickly forgotten. But if we help children understand that the relationship between size and pitch is true for all objects and materials, all the time, everywhere—then those children will be more likely to look for, recognize, and understand other proportional relationships.

Music activities are a natural way to include science education in your curriculum. Young children have already had many positive experiences with music and respond enthusiastically to music activities. And they have abundant curiosity about music and sounds of every kind. They're eager to investigate what music and sound are all about.

How to Use This Book

I have tried to keep the materials needed for these science experiences to a minimum. Most of the activities require very few, and many require none at all. You can find the music suggested in the activities by browsing music-purchasing websites or mobile apps for Apple or Android devices. The emphasis is on helping children to use their own brains and bodies to solve problems, such as "Why did that happen?" and "How could we make this happen?"

I've arranged the activities in *Exploring the Science of Sounds* in learning areas, beginning with an area in which children have a strong knowledge base—the sounds of their own bodies. The next area explores the basics of how sound moves—information students will need to understand the concepts introduced in the following sections. After exploring the sound quality, or timbre, of a variety of objects played in different ways, we move on to the other elements of music. Students further investigate the concepts of time, distance, force, size, and vibration in the sections on loudness, tempo, and pitch. We leave the classroom to explore sounds in the world outside. Finally, children build their own instruments from natural and recycled materials, extending their understanding of the science of sounds and adding their own creativity and individuality.

These areas flow in a meaningful sequence, but you certainly don't need to lead them in order. The activities are a resource for you as you support your students' emerging scientific curiosity. For instance, a child may ask why cymbals are so loud. That's a cue to help the class explore loudness, and you'll want to go to activities in that area to help the class discover for themselves that it isn't the instrument itself that's loud—it depends on how forcefully you play it. (And they'll even discover that

Exploring the Science of Sounds: 100 Musical Activities for Young Children

they can make soft sounds with the cymbals, too.) Your students' interests and curiosity should be your guide.

And one more thing—I'll remind you about this throughout the book, because I find I need to keep reminding myself—take your time. If you ask a question about what children observed or heard or what they predict, and you get one or two responses, wait. Then ask, "Does anyone else have any ideas?" Repeat the original question—maybe in a different wording—and wait some more. There will be more responses. Don't be afraid of a little silence. Silence can be the sound of children thinking.

CHAPTER ONE

THE SOUNDS OF OUR BODIES

Ask the children to think for a minute (without saying anything yet) about sounds they can make with their bodies. After a short time, ask them to raise their hands if they can make a sound with their bodies for the class to hear. Some may clap their hands, stomp their feet, pat their legs, or make other familiar body sounds. Some may make unusual sounds right off the bat. Acknowledge each response with a nod, an *okay* or a *thank you*.

KEY CONCEPT

Different parts of our bodies make different sounds, and we can make more sounds by moving parts of our bodies in different ways.

Sometimes young children don't think of talking, singing, or other vocal sounds as body sounds—it's as if these sounds are in a different category for them. If no one mentions vocal sounds, lead them with questions, such as "What's a sound that we make all day long? What sound am I making right now?" They may protest that talking is different from body sounds, and that's a great topic to discuss. How is it different? How is it the same? What about other vocal sounds?

Tell the group that we will be exploring lots of sounds that our bodies can make—and they may discover new sounds they've never thought of before!

Pa-pum, pa-pum, pa-pum, pa-pum . . . The very first sound we hear, the first thing we're conscious of, is our mother's heartbeat. And as we go through life, the beating of our own hearts is always with us. It's truly the rhythm of life. Since the heartbeat is a major intersection of biology and music, let's begin our exploration here.

What You'll Need

Children's stethoscope

Activity to Try

1. Sing a familiar song, such as "Twinkle, Twinkle, Little Star" with the group. Then sing it again, and have everyone clap to the beat.

2. Tell the children that, just as music has a beat, there's also a beat inside their body that never stops. Do they know what it is? Some will know the answer–our heartbeat. Explain that our hearts pump blood through our bodies to keep us healthy, and the pumping sound has a steady beat. We can feel our heart beating by pressing our right palm over our heart, just slightly left of the center of the chest. (It's even easier to feel it if we place our left hand on top of the right one.) Ask the children to try it, reminding them to be very quiet so everyone can concentrate.

3. Ask what their heartbeats feel like. You might hear responses, such as "It was like a *boom, boom, boom*." "Like a bumping sound." "I couldn't feel anything." All responses are okay.

4. Bring out the stethoscope, and ask the children if they know what it is. They may not know the name, but most will recognize it from doctor visits. Explain that it's a stethoscope, a special device for listening to a heartbeat.

5. Show the child on your right how to listen to your heartbeat with the stethoscope. (I start with my own heartbeat since I know how to find it easily.) Can she hear it? Then help her to listen to her own. Ask her to keep the same beat by patting her chest over her heart when she removes the stethoscope. Have her pass the stethoscope to the child on her right, and continue until all the children in the circle are patting their heartbeats. This activity is very special for young children–I love to see their delighted smiles when they hear their heartbeats!

Questions to Ask

- What did you think your heartbeat would sound like?

- Did your heartbeat sound the way you thought it would? Sometimes each child in the room will want to tell me how their heartbeat sounded. If they want to, I make it a point to listen to every one of them. They're orally representing their observations, and I don't want to brush that off or seem like I don't have time to listen. Acknowledging their observations is a great way to start off our scientific explorations!

- Did it remind you of any other sound you've heard?
- Did your heartbeat go fast and then slow?
- Did it start and stop, or did it have a steady beat?
- Did you hear a little space between beats, like (demonstrate with hand over heart) *pa-pum* (pause) *pa-pum* (pause) *pa-pum*? When children say they did, tell them that means a beat is a pattern–beat/pause, beat/pause, beat/pause, and so on. Pattern is one of the crosscutting concepts that relate to all domains of science.

TIP

Make the stethoscope available during free-play time. The children can use it (with supervision) to listen to their own and each other's heartbeats.

Discoveries to Make

- Hearts make a sound–the heartbeat.
- Children can feel their heartbeats, and they can hear them by using a stethoscope.
- The heartbeat is a steady, regular beat, and a beat is a kind of pattern.

 SOUNDS WE CAN MAKE WITH OUR VOICES

The heartbeat, the most basic sound of the human body, is made by an involuntary movement. When it comes to voluntary sounds, the most common are talking and singing. But these two sounds aren't the whole story. Our voices can make all kinds of sounds, and children love to explore them.

What You'll Need

No materials needed

Activity to Try

1. Tell the class that you'll be exploring all the sounds humans can make with our voices. For instance, right now you're talking–that's a sound you make with your voice. Ask the children if they know other vocal sounds. Some may say singing, but before that, they may think of other sounds, such as humming, growling, sighing, and so on.

2. Go around the circle and have each child make whatever sound they would like to with his voice. Remind them the sounds can be loud or soft, short or long, beautiful or funny—whatever they want. If they copy another child's sound, that's okay. If they make a sound such as clicking their tongue, that isn't, strictly speaking, a vocal sound, but that's okay too. For now, the idea is for children to explore freely and think about the many ways we can use our voices to create sounds.

TIP

Sometimes young children enjoy making sounds, such as squeaks and other extremely high, low, or loud sounds. Let them try these once, but explain that making these sounds too often can make their throats feel sore.

Questions to Ask

- Had you heard all of these sounds before?
- Which ones do you think were the strangest sounds?
- Did anyone think their sound was difficult to make?
- Do you think we can make a lot of sounds with our voices, or only a few sounds? Why do you think so?

Discovery to Make

Children can make many different sounds using their voices.

 WAYS WE CAN CLAP OUR HANDS

"If you're happy and you know it . . ." It's no coincidence that one of the most-loved children's songs begins with clapping. Young children love to clap their hands, and it's a natural response to listening to music, especially when there's a strong beat. They also love to invent new ways to clap. I've been teaching for a long time, and my students still find ways to clap their hands that I've never seen before! This activity harnesses that creative energy to study the sounds produced by various styles of clapping.

What You'll Need

A recording of music with a steady beat (See Suggested Recordings of Instrumental Music on page 190.)

Activity to Try

1. Tell the group that this activity is about clapping our hands. You're going to put on some music, and they're going to clap to the beat of the music together.

2. Put on the music, and play it loud enough for children to hear but soft enough that they can hear you speak over it. Begin clapping.

3. After a while, ask the children to copy you as you clap in different ways. Try clapping high above your head, with your arms held straight out in front of you like a seal, and to the left and the right.

4. Pause the music and ask the children to think of new ways to clap their hands. Explain that when you start the music again, if they have an idea, they should raise their hand quietly and wait to be called on.

5. Start the music again, and let the children show you their clapping ideas. Have the whole class try out each idea. They'll usually come up with lots of ideas, but if they get stuck, show them another way to clap to jump-start their imaginations again. You might clap with your hands held horizontally (one on top of another), behind your back, or with your fingers splayed out. Then challenge them to think of some more ways to clap.

6. If the music stops before the ideas stop flowing, play it again from the beginning. Generate as many ways to clap as you can!

Questions to Ask

- I don't think I could ever have thought of all those ideas by myself! Do you think you could have?

- Do you think we could come up with more ways to clap if we did this all day?

- When we clap our hands, do we also move other parts of our bodies, or only our hands?

- (We move our wrists, our arms, our elbows, and our shoulders. If children aren't sure, have them watch you as you clap and observe which parts of your body are moving. Explain that the body works as a system, because the parts of our body are all related and connected.)

TIP

Encourage the children to respect each other's ideas by thanking each child for her contribution. Always emphasize that everyone's ideas are valuable, and we all learn more by sharing our own and listening to others' ideas.

Discoveries to Make

- Children can clap their hands in many different ways.

- Children can think of more ideas as a group than they can individually.

- Hands can move in many ways because they are attached to wrists, elbows, arms, and shoulders, which can all move in various directions.

- The body is a system made up of parts that are connected and related. (Systems and system models are a crosscutting concept that relate to all domains of science.)

ONE FOOT, TWO FEET

When we think of feet moving, we generally think of walking, running, or dancing rather than creating music or sound. But sounds we make with our feet can be very musical and expressive. For instance, tap dancing isn't just fun to watch, it exploits the sounds of tapping, sliding, and stomping feet for dramatic and musical effect. And no suspense movie would be the same without the sound of footsteps on the stairs. This activity helps children explore not only the sounds they can create with their feet but also the difference in sound when we use one foot compared to two feet.

What You'll Need

No materials needed

Activity to Try

1. The children should be standing. Tell them that you'll be exploring all the sounds you can make with your feet. How about the sound of walking in place? Have the class try it for a few moments. Then ask them to try running in place. Did it sound the same? Why not? Children may notice that it sounded faster and louder.

2. Ask the children what other sounds people can make with our feet. Have the group try out individual children's suggestions. They may try tiptoeing, marching, stomping, sliding, tapping toes, tapping heels, rocking from heels to toes, tapping the side of one foot against the other, hopping, jumping, and more.

3. Ask which sounds can be made by both one foot and two feet. For example, you can slide one foot to the front and back or side to side, and you can also slide both feet by sliding one forward while the other one slides back. Have children compare the sound of one foot sliding with the sound of two feet sliding. (They'll notice that sliding two feet is louder.) Try this with tapping toes, tapping heels, rocking heel to toe, and hopping or jumping. Children can also extend their legs while sitting and use one, and then two, feet for stepping and stomping.

Questions to Ask

- Could we make as many sounds with our feet as we did with our hands? Why not?
- Did we make louder sounds when we did the same movement with one foot or with two feet?
- Could we try some of these sounds using three feet? How? (They could use three feet by adding a foot from another child.)
- Would you say that you can make a louder sound stomping with two feet (while sitting down with legs out) than you can with one foot?
- Can we make a louder sound with three feet than with two feet?

Discoveries to Make

- Children can make many different sounds with their feet.
- Two feet will sound louder than one foot, if they're making the same movement.

> ### KEEP THE LEARNING GOING!
>
> Children may want to see whether four feet (two children's feet) will make an even louder sound than three feet. They may want to go further and try five, six, and seven feet, and so on. Encourage the children to try as many feet as they want. They're on their way to generalizing the rule that more things making the same sound will create a louder sound—in other words, that there is a direct proportional relationship between the two. This relates to the crosscutting concepts of scale, proportion, and quantity, which relate to all domains of science.

SNAPPING, KNUCKLES, NAILS, AND MORE

Hands down (pun intended), hands are the most versatile parts of the body when it comes to moving and creating sound. We've already found that our hands can clap in an almost endless variety of ways. But clapping is just the beginning. Our fingers can make a unique snapping sound, our knuckles can sharply knock on doors or rap on tables, and our nails are perfect scratchers and scrapers. These sounds add to the body's expressive musical repertoire—and also inspire curiosity. How do these parts of our hands create these interesting sounds?

What You'll Need

No materials needed

Activity to Try

1. Review some of the clapping techniques the class discovered, then ask if there are any other sounds we can make using our hands. Most young children will think of snapping fingers, knocking with their knuckles, and scratching with fingernails.
2. Encourage them to keep thinking—what else could we do? If they get stuck, ask leading questions such as, "Could we snap with different fingers against our thumbs?" "Could we knock with just one knuckle?" and "Does rubbing our palms against each other make a sound?" Questions like this inspire the children to think in different directions.

3. Try out the children's ideas together. Continue listening to children's ideas—and inviting the whole group to try out the ideas—for as long as the children have ideas to contribute.

TIP

These questions help children to compare the structures of hands and feet. Let them take their time in thinking this through. Comparison is an important analytical skill, and structure and function are crosscutting concepts that apply across all scientific domains.

Questions to Ask

- We made so many different kinds of sounds. Do you think we could make this many sounds using our feet?

- How are our feet different from our hands?

- Can you snap your toes? How are toes different from fingers?

- What are some of the reasons our hands can make so many different sounds?

Discoveries to Make

- In addition to clapping, we can make many different sounds using our hands.

- Hands have unique features, such as long fingers and knuckles that bend easily, which make it possible for them to make many sounds.

WRONG ANSWERS?

What if children respond to your questions in unexpected ways? (This can pretty much be guaranteed in any preschool group!) What if a child insists that he can snap his toes? Resist the urge to correct him. Affirm his thinking process by saying something like, "That's an interesting idea. Let's try it." Children love an opportunity to try something new and tricky. One group I taught was determined to show me they could snap their toes. They rubbed their big toes against their second toes and told me their toes were snapping! (Although they did admit it sounded different from fingers snapping.)

SOUNDS WE CAN MAKE USING ONLY OUR LIPS, TEETH, AND TONGUES

Long before young children learn to talk, they explore all kinds of ways to make sounds with their mouths. They babble, coo, and blow "raspberries" with their soft lips. Mouth sounds continue to interest them throughout early childhood. Here, we share these sounds and stretch our imaginations, thinking up even more nonvocal sounds to make with our mouths.

What You'll Need

Dry-erase board or large piece of paper

Dry-erase marker or regular marker

Activity to Try

1. Tell the class that you'll be exploring all the sounds you can make using only your lips, teeth, and tongues. First have them think about sounds they can make with their lips. They'll probably suggest popping their lips, making kissing sounds, and variations on these. They may say humming, which I accept, since we couldn't hum without our lips, although it does use our voices also.

2. Ask whether they could make more sounds using their hands and their lips together. (If no one comes up with this, show them how to make a long oval with your open mouth and clap your straight hand gently on your lips for a hollow, echoey sound. Then experiment—does it sound the same with your lips closed?)

3. Ask the children for teeth sounds. They might think of tapping or chattering their teeth together and making the /ch/ sound. (Technically, this also uses the tongue.)

4. Ask the children for tongue sounds. They'll definitely click their tongues. Some will get creative and try making sounds with their tongues rolled—smacking their lips around them, blowing through them, or "thooping" their upper teeth over them. It can get pretty silly and fun as children watch each other making these sounds!

5. Make a chart with all the sounds written out and/or illustrated. Children love to come up to the chart and make illustrations. You can even lead the class in a performance in which they make the mouth sounds you point to on the chart—they'll think this is hilarious. Keep the chart posted on the wall for the class to play the "point and play" game on their own.

Questions to Ask

- Did all the sounds you made sound the same?
- How do your lips feel? Soft or hard? Smooth or scratchy?
- How do your teeth feel?
- How does your tongue feel?
- Do you think your lips, teeth, and tongue are all made out of the same stuff?

Discoveries to Make

- Children can make many different sounds with their lips, teeth, and tongues.
- Lips, teeth, and tongues make different kinds of sounds because they're made of different kinds of material. (If anyone asks what they're made of, you can tell them that lips are made of skin and muscle, the tongue is mostly muscle, and each tooth has something called pulp on the inside, then dentin (like bone) covering the pulp, and a hard enamel covering the outside.)

WHAT ARE THEY DOING IN THERE?

In other activities in this section, children explore many ways to make sounds using their voices, hands, feet, lips, teeth, and tongues. Now it's time to apply all that knowledge and have some fun. You'll be playing games using body sounds that involve active listening, following verbal directions and musical cues, and problem-solving. Here, children will solve a mystery—identifying a sound when they can't see how it's being made.

What You'll Need

A small blanket, large enough to cover one child

Activity to Try

1. Tell the children you're about to make a sound. Then click your tongue and ask them what sound you made. After they identify this sound, tell them that it's easy to know what a sound is when you can see the person making that sound. But what if you can't see the person? Do they think identifying the sound would still be so easy?

2. Explain that one child will go under the blanket and make a sound—any of the sounds you've learned about using your voices, hands, feet, lips, teeth, or tongues. Then, another child will try to guess the sound the child under the blanket is making.

3. Ask a child to sit in the middle of the circle. Hide the child under the blanket and ask her to stay there for a moment. Then ask another child to be the guesser. Remind the children that only the guesser will guess the sound. Everyone else should just think about their answer, without saying it aloud.

4. Have the first child make a sound, and have the guesser guess what sound it is. (I usually let children have three tries in guessing games to give them a better chance of being correct.) If the guesser cannot guess the sound, let another child try.

5. When the guesser guesses the sound (or no one does), choose another child to hide under the blanket and make a sound.

6. Continue the game until everyone in the circle has had a turn to either make a sound or guess a sound.

> **TIP**
>
> If it's hard for the children to keep quiet and let the guesser guess the sound, you can try having them hold a finger in front of their mouths as if they're reminding someone to be quiet. After the game, remember to congratulate everyone for using their self-control.

Questions to Ask

- Did you think this game would be easy or hard? Were you right?
- What if there were two people under the blanket making the same sound—do you think it would be easier to guess the sound? Why? (If they want, they could try this out.)
- What if the two people were making different sounds? Do you think it would be harder to guess the two sounds? Why?
- How did you guess what sound the person was making?

Discovery to Make

Children can correctly identify a sound using only their hearing.

 HERE COMES THE BEAT

The benefits of being able to keep a steady beat go way beyond playing a musical instrument or looking good on the dance floor. Researchers Adam Tierney and Nina Kraus have linked this ability to language skills, and it also has been linked to emergent math skills, since beats in music are arranged in repeated patterns. You can help your students develop this ability every day by clapping or patting thighs to familiar songs and nursery rhymes. The following activity also hones this skill, using all the body sounds the children have learned.

What You'll Need

A recording of music with a steady beat (See "Suggested Recordings of Instrumental Music" on page 190.)

Activity to Try

1. Ask the children to think back over all the sounds they have made with their bodies. Explain that you're going to play a game in which you keep the beat of the music using these body sounds.

2. Start the music. First, children should copy your sounds as you keep the beat for half a minute or so. Keep changing the way you keep the beat, from clapping to tongue-clicking to tapping your shoulders, and so on. Switch sounds at a pace slow enough for the children to follow along easily.

3. Pause the music and ask if anyone else would like to lead the game. Continue until all the children who want to lead have had a turn.

TIP

Playing "Here Comes the Beat" several times over a period of a few weeks reinforces children's ability to keep a steady beat. It also gives everyone an opportunity to lead the group, even those children who may have been hesitant the first time around.

Questions to Ask

- Can you tell me some of the ways we kept the beat?

- The beat of the music keeps it moving at a steady pace. Do you remember the part of your body that keeps your blood moving through your body at a steady pace?

- Do we need to play musical instruments to keep the beat when we're listening to music?

Discoveries to Make

- Children can keep a steady beat using only body sounds.

- Children can lead a musical activity independently, without a teacher's help.

CLICKER BUGS AND POPPER BUGS

Two of the "mouth sounds" we explore are always big favorites with young children: tongue clicking and lip popping. They're not very complicated movements, but they're just difficult enough so that children see them as tricks and feel proud of doing them well. I brought these two sounds together for this silly, fun game based on the general idea of "Duck, Duck, Goose."

What You'll Need

1 small hand drum or tambourine

Activity to Try

1. Tell the children that in this game they're all going to pretend to be bugs. Put them into two groups. The easiest way to do this is simply to split the circle into two halves, one half seated on your left and one half on your right.

2. Tell the group on the left that they're going to pretend to be special imaginary bugs called clicker bugs. They're called clicker bugs because they make a clicking sound. (Click your tongue to demonstrate.) Ask the "clicker bugs" to try making that sound.

3. Tell the group on your right that they'll be popper bugs—they make a popping sound. (Pop your lips to demonstrate.) Have the "popper bugs" make that sound. Now they're ready to play.

4. Explain that you will beat on your drum (or tambourine) slowly and say the word *ladybug* on each beat. But sometimes you'll say a different word. You might say *clicker bug*—then the "clicker bugs" have to make their special sound. Or you might say *popper bug*—that means it's time for the "popper bugs" to pop! Remind them that they will have to really concentrate to listen for the name of their bug.

5. Start the game. Vary the number of times you say *ladybug* to keep the children alert.

6. After the game is over (a minute is usually plenty), congratulate the children on their excellent concentration.

7. Play again, with the "clicker bugs" and "popper bugs" switching roles.

Questions to Ask

- Did I ever catch you by surprise? When?
- After a while, did your tongue get tired from clicking? Did your lips get tired from popping?
- Would this game be easier if I said only *clicker bug* and *popper bug*, without saying *ladybug* in between?
- Do you think you could play this game with your eyes closed? How do you know? (If they're not sure, try it!)

> **TIP**
>
> To make the game even trickier, say the names of a variety of bugs, such as *spider*, *bumblebee*, *ant*, and so on—in between *clicker bug* and *popper bug*.

Discoveries to Make

- Children can focus their listening to follow verbal directions, even when those directions are "hidden" among other words.
- Children need only their ears, not their eyes, to follow spoken directions.

 THE SNAKE AND THE CAKE

We've explored all kinds of body sounds, and we've practiced them in two different games. This activity brings in a new element—using body sounds to dramatize a story.

What You'll Need

No materials needed

Activity to Try

1. Ask the group what a movie would be like if it had only words and pictures, with no sounds or music. It would be pretty boring, wouldn't it? Music and sounds add a lot of fun and excitement to stories.
2. Tell the children they're going to help you make sounds for a short, silly rhyme that tells a story. Have them practice the sounds: the hiss of a snake, the "mmmmm" sound of someone tasting something yummy, patting their thighs for when we're talking about their laps, and a yawn to show that someone is sleepy.

3. Introduce the rhyme:

> *There once was a snake, (hisssss)*
> *And she ate a piece of cake. (mmmmm)*
> *Then she crawled on my lap, (pat, pat, pat)*
> *And she took a little nap. (yawwwn)*
> *She woke up from the nap, (yawwwn)*
> *And she crawled off my lap. (pat, pat, pat)*
> *She looked for more cake. (mmmmm)*
> *What a silly little snake! (hisssss)*

4. Have the children join in with the noises as you repeat the chant slowly.
5. Invite the class to try the chant a little faster.
6. Repeat twice more, until it's really fast.

Questions to Ask

- Who can tell me all the sounds we made for this little story?
- Would this story be as silly and fun without making the sounds? If the children aren't sure, try it again, without the sounds.
- How did the sounds we made with our bodies help to tell the story?

Discoveries to Make

- Children can use body sounds to help dramatize a story to make it more fun and interesting.
- Sounds can actually help to tell a story. For instance, when we made the sound "mmmmm," we showed that the snake enjoyed eating the cake.

KEEP THE LEARNING GOING!

During transitions or while they are waiting to be picked up, have the children try making body sounds to dramatize familiar songs and rhymes. For instance, in "The Wheels on the Bus," ask them what sound they could make after the word *bus*. (Maybe they could make a *vroom vroom* sound.)

ONCE UPON A TAP

Now we're going beyond body sounds to use tapping sounds. To make it more fun, it's a memory game, so we need to keep all the previous sounds in mind. (My students love playing these kinds of games with me, since I invariably forget sounds before they do. It's always fun to beat a grown-up at a game!)

What You'll Need

No materials needed

Activity to Try

1. Tell the class you're going to play a game about tapping different parts of the body. Explain that it's a memory game.

2. Say the following chant and demonstrate the motions.

> *Once upon a tap,*
> *I tapped my head, 1, 2, 3.* (Tap head with a pointer finger)
> *Once upon a tap,*
> *I tapped my head, 1, 2, 3.* (Tap head with a pointer finger)
> *And then I tapped my knee, 1, 2, 3.* (Tap knee with a pointer finger)

3. Explain that the children will take turns adding new tapping sounds to the game.

4. Ask a child to have the first turn. Repeat the chant, and then the child can add another part of the body to tap.

5. Repeat, going around the circle, asking each child to add a tapping sound, until it gets too hard for most children to remember all the previous sounds.

Questions to Ask

- Did you think this game was as easy as most games, or a little bit harder? I use this phrasing because some children react to the question, "Was it easy or hard?" by assuring me they found it easy. Many children don't like to admit something is hard.

- Why do you think it was a little bit harder?

- Can you think of more ways to tap that we didn't do yet? Because the game is limited by how many sounds they can remember, some children who didn't get a turn will want to share their ideas.
- I want you to think about this for a minute before you answer. Can we tap many parts of the body, or just a few parts? I often say the "right" answer first since many children—and adults—automatically answer with the last alternative when they're not sure.

Discovery to Make

Children can tap many parts of the body to make sounds.

TIP

Don't let the children off too easy! Encourage them to try to tap body parts they haven't tried before. Some of my students have suggested tapping eyebrows, bellybuttons, each of the individual fingers, wrists, heels, foreheads, chins, and hips!

ADDING BODY SOUNDS TO THE SONG "IF YOU'RE HAPPY AND YOU KNOW IT"

I'm going to tell you a secret. (Please don't tell anyone.) I don't like "Old MacDonald Had a Farm." I sing it because young children love it, but I'm just not a fan. When I was a preschooler, "If You're Happy and You Know It" and "Itsy Bitsy Spider" were my favorite songs, and I love them to this day. The big dramatic gesture on "washed the spider out" is so satisfying, and I always get into the rhythm of "If You're Happy and You Know It." The structure of the song lends itself to zippering in all kinds of sounds and movements.

What You'll Need

Dry-erase easel or large paper and marker

Activity to Try

1. Sing "If You're Happy and You Know It" with the usual verses.

> ### TIP
>
> Many young children will offer suggestions nonverbally. Preschoolers show a wide range of language proficiency, and some sounds and movements are difficult for anyone to quickly express in words. For instance, they might snap their fingers while waving alternating hands up and down. If an idea simply won't fit rhythmically into the song, you can sing, "If you're happy and you know it, go like this." This will help you keep the activity moving along, rather than getting bogged down in how to describe the sound and movement.

2. Ask the children to pop their lips if they're happy and they know it!

> *If you're happy and you know it, pop your lips. (pop pop) . . .*

3. Sing a few other verses, maybe with knocking your elbows together or scratching your head. By making varied sounds, you'll inspire a broader range of ideas from the children. Hands will start shooting up with great suggestions before you know it! Try to give every child a turn if time permits.

Questions to Ask

- Do you remember all the parts of the body we used to make sounds in this song? List them as children remember them.
- Did we use any instruments to make the sounds?
- Did we need a phone or another device to sing this song and make all the sounds?

Discovery to Make

Children can produce a variety of musical sounds to accompany a song using only their bodies.

USING BODY SOUNDS TO ACCOMPANY A STORY

When children can make sounds to help dramatize a story as you read, it increases their engagement and focus enormously. Sounds enrich the experience of read-alouds and heighten the humor or drama of the action. Children wait eagerly for the next cue to meow, stamp their feet like elephants, or click their tongues to cluck like chickens. In this activity, children use more than sounds—they use their brains to decide which sounds to use at various points in a story.

What You'll Need

A picture book that mentions many sounds, such as *The Fox in the Dark* by Alison Green, *Big Wolf and Little Wolf* by Sharon Phillips Denslow, *The Leopard's Drum* by Jessica Souhami, or *Fire! Fire! Hurry! Hurry!* by Andrea Zimmerman and David Clemesha

Activity to Try

1. This is a two-day activity. On the first day, read the story. Introduce it by asking the children to be thinking about sounds they could make using their bodies, to help tell the story when you read it again tomorrow. Explain that they might use animal sounds, walking or running sounds, or they could use their bodies to sound like creaking wood or sirens.

2. On the second day, review the story page by page, and ask the children for ideas for sounds to go with the action on each page. Give as many children as possible an opportunity to contribute. This may involve expanding the story quite a bit—for instance, you could ask for a sound to be the leaves of a tree rustling in the wind or a mouse's tiny feet pitter-pattering. Or several children could make one sound together.

3. Review the sounds the children will make and the cues. For example, when you read the word drum, they'd make their drum sound.

4. Read the story again, with the children adding their sounds.

Questions to Ask

- What did you think was different about reading the story with all the sounds in it? Was it more exciting and fun?

- Which part of the story was the hardest to think of a sound for?

- How did you decide which sound would go best with each part of the story?

Discovery to Make

Children can make connections between sounds they've heard and sounds they can make with their bodies, to help tell a story and make it more fun and interesting.

TIP

Children's ideas for sounds to portray characters and actions may be very different from what you'd expect. Rather than leading them to more "reasonable," conventional sounds, accept their ideas. Your positive response will affirm their problem-solving abilities and make them excited about tackling new problems.

CHAPTER TWO

HOW SOUND MOVES: THE SCIENCE OF ACOUSTICS

Ask the children whether they've ever wondered what music is and where it comes from. What do they think music is? Children usually have many sensible answers, such as "It's like a song," "Music is when you play an instrument," "It's when you listen to the radio," and even "Music is everywhere." Be sure to listen to every child who wants to offer an opinion, and then tell the group that those were all good answers. They all told you something about what music is.

Discuss what they'd like to know about music. There might not be a lot of responses at this point, since they've just started thinking about the subject, but some children will have particular things they're wondering about.

Tell the class that you'll be exploring all about what music is. You'll do experiments and find out how music works, where it comes from, how it starts and stops, and you'll even find out if it's possible to see music and sound!

KEY CONCEPTS

- Sounds are vibrations.

- Sound can move through air, water, and solid objects.

SOUNDS ARE VIBRATIONS

Since I started exploring tuning forks with young children, I've been more and more excited about the educational possibilities. Children are amazed right off the bat when they see the tuning fork being struck and hear its clear, sharp tone. They're even more excited when they touch the tuning fork as it's vibrating. Listening to the vibrating tuning fork as it touches guitars, drums, and any other instrument or object is fascinating, too. They'll want to try it on everything they see. (And they should.) Every classroom should have a tuning fork!

What You'll Need

1 tuning fork, at least 7" long for the best effect. I use a C-256 Hz tuning fork.

A mallet, such as a glockenspiel mallet

Activity to Try

1. Show the class the tuning fork. Can they guess what it is? Listen to the children's ideas.

2. Tell them it's called a tuning fork and that it's a special device used by musicians. The tuning fork always makes the same clear tone, so they can make sure their instruments sound right. Scientists use tuning forks too, to study how sound works. It's made of metal and it vibrates, or moves quickly back and forth, when you hit it, playing a musical tone.

3. Hit the tuning fork hard with a mallet. Ask the class whether they can observe it moving. (They'll say no, and wonder how it's making the sound.)

4. Explain that even though you can't see it, the tuning fork vibrates when you strike it—it moves back and forth really, really fast, like this (hold up your forearm and vibrate it quickly). It vibrates so fast that it makes the air vibrate. The vibrations keep moving through the air, so our ears hear the sound.

5. Go around the circle to show each child how the tuning fork works. For every child, hit the fork, then hold it next to the child's ear so she can hear how the sound continues for quite a while. While the fork is still ringing, let her touch the end of one of the tines. She'll feel a small but very noticeable buzz—a zapping, tingling feeling. It's the tuning fork vibrating. Every child I've worked with has been fascinated and delighted by this experience.

6. Remind the children that we hear that tone and feel that buzz because when we hit the tuning fork it makes music by vibrating. (You can demonstrate with your forearm again.) Those vibrations are what music is made of—all sounds come from vibrations.

Questions to Ask

- What did the tuning fork feel like when it was vibrating?
- Do you think that there's any way we might be able to see the vibrations of sound?
- Does the tuning fork vibrate by itself?
- What has to happen for it to start vibrating and making sound?

Discoveries to Make

- A tuning fork is an instrument used by musicians and scientists that always produces the same clear tone.
- Striking the tuning fork causes it to vibrate, or move back and forth very fast. This creates the ringing tone.
- The vibration of the tuning fork is so strong, we can feel it "buzzing" when we touch it.

KEEP THE LEARNING GOING!

Over the next few days, keep the tuning fork with you and show your class how striking it and touching the ringing fork to various objects produces sounds. Guitars, drums, and other hollow items will be particularly resonant, but lots of things will have interesting sounds. Have children compare the various sounds. Bring out the tuning fork occasionally during free-play time and let children use it (always with supervision).

CAN WE SEE SOUND MOVING?

Children can hear music and other sounds, but sometimes it's hard for them to really wrap their heads around something unless they can see it. In fact, a boy once asked me, "How do we know music is real if we can't see it?" Well, we can't exactly see music, but we can see its effects in this fascinating examination of how sound moves in water.

What You'll Need

Tuning fork

Mallet

Clear plastic cup

Full water bottle

Newspaper

Activity to Try

1. Tell the class that you can hear sound, and you're going to find out whether you can see it, too! Lay the newspaper on the floor in the middle of the circle or on a table that all the children can gather around. Set the cup in the middle, and fill it with water to very near the top.

2. Explain that we know that sound can move through air, but water is a liquid (a substance that can be poured easily). Ask the children if they think sound will move through this liquid. Listen to their answers.

3. Hit the tuning fork with the mallet very sharply. (I find that striking near the top of one of the tines, on a corner edge, works best.) Touch the fork's tines to the surface of the water. Hold it with the tines almost horizontal (think of an airplane touching down) for best results. Touch only the water—make sure you don't hit the rim of the cup; that will stop the vibration.

4. The water will vibrate, fizz, and splash out onto the newspaper. This always gets a lot of oohs, giggles, and shrieks! Ask the children whether they all saw the water vibrating and splashing. If not, have children move around and do the demonstration again to let all the children have a good look. The children will probably want to try this themselves. If they want to and you have the time, let them! (Always with your supervision.)

5. Did the children see sound move? Well, kind of. What they saw was the water moving because the vibration of sound was moving through it. But rather than just telling this to the class, let them "think out loud," discussing whether or not they actually saw sound. When the argument comes to a standstill, tell them they'll know more as you do more exploring on how sound moves.

Questions to Ask

- What did the water do when we touched it with the tuning fork?
- Why did the water move?
- Were the sound vibrations moving through the water?
- Did we see sound moving?

Discoveries to Make

- The vibration of sound can move through water.
- Water is a liquid, a type of substance that can be poured easily.

KEEP THE LEARNING GOING!

Ask the children whether they know of any other liquids. They may suggest milk, juice, and soda. Challenge them with a question, such as "What about paper? Is paper a liquid? Why not?" They'll tell you that because it can't be poured easily, it's not a liquid.

VIBRATION–A SPECIAL KIND OF MOTION

In their observations of the tuning fork in the "Can We See Sound Moving?" activity, children noticed the fork moving after it was hit against something. You briefly mentioned that this kind of motion (moving back and forth quickly) is called vibration. All sound stems from vibrations. In this activity, you'll explore ways other objects and musical instruments can be used to create vibrations and make sounds.

What You'll Need

Large, strong rubber bands

Stringed instrument, such as a ukulele or a guitar

Activity to Try

1. Remind the children of what they observed in the "Can We See Sound Moving?" activity. They saw the tuning fork's movements, called vibrations, make the water move. Explain that they will find out if they can see sound vibrations in other objects and musical instruments.

2. Show the children a large rubber band. Ask them whether they think it will make a sound if you hold it between your hands fairly tightly and someone plucks it. Listen to several answers, being sure to ask the children why they believe the rubber band will or won't make a sound. Most likely, they'll rely on previous knowledge of rubber bands to predict that this one will make a sound.

3. Hold the rubber band stretched between your hands, and ask a nearby child to pluck it. You can invite the other children to gather close to listen, since it might make a rather soft sound.

4. Acknowledge that the rubber band did make a sound. Ask the children what else it did. You might ask if it moved. At this point, the children may not be sure, since they were paying attention to the sound, not the motion.

5. Try the plucking again, asking the children first to watch the movement of the rubber band. Then you might ask, "Did it move? How did it move?" They may show you with their fingers how the rubber band moved quickly back and forth.

6. Bring out a guitar or ukulele. Ask them whether they think the guitar strings will move like the rubber band did. After hearing the children's answers and the reasoning behind their answers, have a child gently but firmly pluck one of the guitar strings. If they look carefully, children will see the guitar string vibrating.

> **TIP**
>
> It's time-consuming, but more learning will happen if every child in the group has a turn to pluck the rubber band and the guitar string. To keep the other children engaged, you could have a small group at each instrument, with charts for them to note whether the rubber band or guitar string vibrates each time it's played. For each child's name, list Yes ___ No ___, and encourage each child to make a check mark in the blank that he thinks is correct.

Questions to Ask

- Were you surprised when the rubber band and the guitar string vibrated?

- Was that what you thought would happen?

- Do you think that all music and sound is caused by vibrations, whether or not you can see the vibrations? Some children will say yes, and some will say they're not sure. That's fine—they've seen only a few examples of sound vibrations. Tell them you will be exploring more sound vibrations in the future.

Discovery to Make

A plucked rubber band and a plucked string on an instrument will vibrate in similar ways.

Exploring the Science of Sounds: 100 Musical Activities for Young Children

LET'S VIBRATE!

This game is very silly and short, but children really like it. It's good for clarifying the difference between vibration and other kinds of movement. One day I was trying to explain vibration to a class, with little success, when I improvised a demonstration. "Say I'm going like this," I said, moving my arm around aimlessly. "I'm moving, but I'm not vibrating. Now watch." I held my arm still, with my forearm bent up, and I jiggled the forearm from left to right as quickly as I could. "That's vibrating." The children thought this was hilarious and made me do it again several times.

What You'll Need

Tambourine or other loud instrument

Activity to Try

1. Ask the children to stand in a circle or spread out if you have enough room.
2. Tell them that when you tap a beat on the tambourine, they can move any way they want, but without vibrating. Show them how to move without vibrating. When you stop tapping and shake the tambourine, that's their signal to stand still and make their arms vibrate. Demonstrate how to vibrate.
3. Play the game. Tap and shake the tambourine, keeping the "vibrating" parts short. Vibrating is fun but tiring!
4. Ask the children to sit down.

> **TIP**
>
> When children are familiar with this game, it makes a great transition activity. Children can take turns leading the activity, tapping the drum to signal that children should move without vibrating, and shaking it when it's time for all the children to vibrate.

Questions to Ask

- Do you remember how sound moves? Does it move in a lot of ways, or does it just vibrate?
- Is vibration a pattern? What do you think?
- How is vibrating different from other kinds of movement?

Discoveries to Make

- Vibration is a repeated back-and-forth motion, different from other kinds of movement.
- Vibration is a pattern—back/forth, back/forth, and so on.

CAN SOUND MOVE THROUGH A SOLID OBJECT?

I love doing this exploration with young children, since it's the first sound experience most of them will have that is truly counterintuitive. Learning through their own explorations that sound can move through a solid object—and will actually sound louder than the same sound heard through the air—doesn't seem to make sense. Open their minds to the possibilities of the natural world.

What You'll Need

Low table

Child-size chair

Activity to Try

1. Remind the children how they discovered that sound moves in the "Sounds Are Vibrations" and "Can We See Sound Moving?" activities. Ask them how sound moves. Some children will remember that sound moves as a vibration, moving quickly back and forth.

2. Ask them whether sound can move through the air. If they're struggling with this, ask them how they can hear people talking. How does the sound get from someone else's mouth to our ears?

3. Ask them whether sound can move through water. They'll remember seeing sound moving through water in the "Can We See Sound Moving?" activity.

4. Ask the children if they think sound could move through a solid thing, such as a table. The response I get most often is a general consensus of "Hmm." Most children haven't thought about this before. But sometimes they'll say, "No, because the table is too hard."

5. Tell them there might be a way to find out. Have everyone move to the low table. Knock on the table with your knuckles, making sure everyone can see you. Ask them if they heard the knock, and how the knocking sound traveled from the table to their ears. Most children will respond, "Through the air."

6. Ask the group if they think they could hear the knock if they leaned over and pressed an ear to the table. Would the sound move right through the table to their ear?

7. Have a child pull up a chair next to you. Ask him to lean his head down and put his ear on the table. Knock again in the same way.

Exploring the Science of Sounds: 100 Musical Activities for Young Children

8. Ask him whether he heard the knock. Probably before you even ask, he'll exclaim excitedly that not only could he hear the sound through the table, but it was much louder!

9. A good way to continue this is to have that child knock for the next child, and so on. That way, each child will have an opportunity to be the "knocker" and the "hearer." Children always want turns at both! After everyone has had turns at both roles, return to the circle.

Questions to Ask

- Were you surprised that you could hear the sound through the table?
- Do you think we could hear sounds through other solid things, such as a door? If they're not sure, have them try it! Have one child knock on a door while another puts her ear to the other side.
- Do you think we could hear other sounds, such as tapping fingers or jingle bells, through the table? Again, children can try out other sounds to find out whether they travel through solids.
- Would you say that sound can move through solid objects?

Discoveries to Make

- Sound can move through solids.
- Sounds are actually louder when heard through solids than through the air.

> "When we find out we're wrong, we start learning."
>
> —John Van Enk, blogger, Atomic Spin

  CRUNCH!

Snack time! It's always a highlight of the school day. It's also a great time to explore how sound travels. Prepare for the children to be amazed!

What You'll Need

Crunchy bite-sized snack, such as small crackers or pretzels, one serving per child

Activity to Try

1. You can present this activity casually during your regular snack time. Ask the children if they've ever listened to the sound they make when they eat crackers. Listen to any responses.

2. Have everyone hold up a cracker. Tell the children, "We're all going to crunch our crackers at the same time. Okay, one–two–three–go!" You and the children should pop the crackers into your mouths and crunch them.

3. Ask how the crackers sounded. Children may respond with words such as *crunchy* and *loud*.

4. Tell them you're thinking of a way that might make cracker eating sound different. Invite them to cover their ears with their hands when they crunch the crackers and to listen to what happens. Do the hands-on-ears crunch with the children and watch their faces—it's a "wow" moment. They'll want to do this a few more times, usually until they're out of crackers.

Questions to Ask

- How was the sound different when you covered your ears?

- Were you crunching harder when your hands covered your ears, or were you crunching the same as the first time?

- Can you think of any reasons why it was so much louder when you covered your ears?

- They'll realize that by covering their ears, they were blocking out the other sounds in the room. They may think this is the only reason the crunching sounded louder. Confirm that this is one reason.

- Do you remember how sound travels most loudly? Is it through gases such as air, liquids such as water, or solids such as the table? They'll remember that sound travels most loudly through solids.

- Are there any solid things inside our heads? Children will realize that there are solids inside our heads, including our bones and teeth.

- Do you think what you hear when you cover your ears could be the sound of crunching traveling through your bones and teeth?

Discoveries to Make

- By covering our ears when eating crunchy food, we can hear the crunching sound traveling through our bones and teeth.

- Sound travels easily and loudly through the solids in our heads.

Children may find it interesting that scientists have studied the way sound travels through our bones, which is called *bone conduction*, to help build new kinds of hearing aids for people who have trouble hearing.

SCRAPING RHYTHM STICKS IN THE AIR AND ON THE FLOOR

Purely by accident, years ago, I made an amazing discovery. I was playing rhythm sticks with a group of four-year-olds, and I tried scraping the sticks in a new way. With the bumpy stick held flat on the hard floor, I scraped it hard with the smooth stick—and whoa! All the children looked up when they heard the sound then tried it themselves. The sound wasn't just loud—it was much, much louder than scraping the sticks above the floor! I've mentioned this phenomenon briefly in an earlier book, but I'm exploring it in more depth here because it perfectly illustrates the dramatic difference between sound traveling through the air and through solids. Plus it's really cool.

What You'll Need

2 rhythm sticks for each child

Dry-erase easel or large paper and marker

Activity to Try

1. Ask the children how sound moves through air, liquids, and solids. (It moves slowly through air, faster through liquids, and very quickly through solids.)

2. Bring out a pair of rhythm sticks, and tell the group that they're going to do an experiment. Write *Experiment* on the easel.

3. Hold the sticks about 6 inches above the floor. Demonstrate how you scrape the bumpy stick with the smooth one to get a raspy sound.

4. Write "1. Question" on the easel. Tell the children the question for this experiment is "Which will sound louder, scraping the sticks in the air or scraping them while holding the bumpy one flat on the floor? Or will they sound the same?" By "1. Question," write the question, or draw a long line to represent the floor, sticks crossed over the floor, and sticks on the floor, followed by a question mark.

5. Ask the children which way they think will be louder, or if they think both ways will sound the same. Have a few children explain the reasoning behind their answers and get a consensus from the group.

6. Ask whether anyone remembers what the word is for "predicting what will happen." At least a few students will remember. Write "2. Hypothesis" on the easel, and write or draw their prediction.

7. Sometimes, a class won't agree on a hypothesis or will simply not be able to predict what will happen. That's fine. You don't want to tell them what to think. Just draw a question mark next to *Hypothesis*.

8. Explain that the next part of the experiment, where you try out both ways to scrape, is called "Testing the Hypothesis." Write "3. Testing the Hypothesis." Tell the children that first, you'll scrape the sticks above the floor, and then you'll scrape them on the floor. Write or draw this on the easel.

9. Place pairs of sticks on the floor in front of each student. They should not pick them up until you say so.

10. Invite the children to scrape the sticks above the floor first and listen to how it sounds.

11. Show children how to hold the bumpy stick by grasping the very tip and holding the stick as flat as they can on the floor. When they're ready, have them scrape the sticks on the floor. When the whole class does this together, it's really, really loud!

Questions to Ask

- Can you describe what you heard? Write "4. Observations" on the easel, and write their comments.
- What's our answer? Was scraping the sticks louder above the ground or on the ground? Tell them the answer is also called the *conclusion* and write "5. Conclusion" on the easel. Write or draw what the class decided.
- Was our hypothesis correct?
- Why do you think that scraping the sticks sounded louder on the floor?

Discoveries to Make

- Sticks scraped on the floor are louder than sticks scraped in the air.
- When children scrape sticks on the floor, the sound vibrations actually travel through the floor.
- Since the floor is a solid, the sound traveled more loudly through it than through the air.

TIP

This experiment is more fun when you can play on a hard floor. If you have carpet, it will absorb some of the sound, and the effect won't be as dramatic. But, children will still hear an obvious difference between scraping in the air and on the floor.

Exploring the Science of Sounds: 100 Musical Activities for Young Children

WHICH WILL SOUND LOUDER: RHYTHM STICKS HITTING A HARD FLOOR OR MITTENS HITTING A HARD FLOOR?

Yes, the answer to this question seems fairly obvious! With this activity, most children will find that their predictions, based on their experiences with these objects, are correct. As you'll see, however, you'll be encouraging the children to really think about the reasoning behind their predictions. Understanding their reasoning processes—and how they can apply them to more difficult problems—is the most important part of this experiment.

What You'll Need

2 rhythm sticks (unsharpened pencils can also be used)

Area with a hard, uncarpeted floor

2 mittens

Activity to Try

1. Bring out the rhythm sticks and the mittens. Explain that you'll be doing an experiment. Tell the children that you're going to hit this hard floor with some rhythm sticks and then hit the floor with the mittens. Ask them to quietly think about this question: Which will sound louder—the sticks hitting the floor or the mittens hitting the floor?

2. Invite children to share their hypotheses and the reasoning behind them. Most will say something like, "The sticks will be louder, because the sticks are hard and the mittens are soft." You don't need to delve further at this point. Confirm that their hypothesis is that the rhythm sticks will sound louder than the mittens.

3. Ask one child to hit the floor with the rhythm sticks and another to hit the floor with the mittens.

4. Ask the class to describe the different sounds.

Questions to Ask

- Were we right when we made the hypothesis that the rhythm sticks would be louder?

- How did you know they would be louder?

- If they repeat that the sticks are hard and the mittens are soft, probe further with questions, such as "What are some other hard things you've heard make a loud sound when they hit the floor?"

- If they're not sure, ask them if they've ever dropped blocks or plastic toys on the floor. This may help them remember other things.

- Have you ever dropped anything soft, such as a sweater, a pillow, or a stuffed animal, on the floor? What did the soft thing sound like?
- Do you think that knowing about all the loud and soft things you've heard hit the floor helped you make the hypothesis that the sticks would be louder than the mittens?

TIP

Thinking about how we think is difficult. Give children plenty of time to talk about hard and soft objects they've heard and how they sounded.

Discoveries to Make

- Sticks make louder sounds than mittens when they're hit on the floor.
- Children are able to make good hypotheses, or predictions about what will happen, by recalling similar things that happened in the past.

WHICH WILL SOUND LOUDER: CYMBALS CRASHING INTO EACH OTHER OR CYMBALS WRAPPED IN SMALL TOWELS AND CRASHING INTO EACH OTHER?

This activity builds on the children's base of knowledge about the relative loudness of hard and soft materials. This time, children will compare the sound of a hard material (metal) with the same hard material covered with a soft material (the fabric of a towel).

What You'll Need

2 pairs of the same size cymbals (or four pot lids of the same size)

2 small towels

Rubber bands

Activity to Try

1. Explain that this experiment is about hard and soft materials. Tell the children that they know two hard things hitting each other will be loud, but will they be as loud if they're covered with a soft material? Listen to their responses.

2. Bring out the two pairs of cymbals. Wrap one pair with the towels, and secure the towels with rubber bands twisted on near the knobs. Ask the class what they think you're going to do. Many hands will shoot up—they can guess that you're going to compare the sounds of the regular cymbals and the towel-covered ones.

3. Confirm that this is exactly what we're going to do, and ask whether anyone remembers what it's called when you predict what will happen. They will know it's a hypothesis. Get a show of hands—how many think the regular cymbals will sound louder? How many think the towel-covered ones will be louder?

4. Count up, and confirm that most people think the regular cymbals will be louder. Tell the children that is the hypothesis.

5. Ask for two children to crash the cymbals. Have one child crash the regular pair and another crash the towel-wrapped pair.

6. Ask the group to describe the sounds they heard.

Questions to Ask

- Which pair of cymbals was louder? Was our hypothesis right?

- How did you know the regular cymbals would be louder? If they reply that cymbals are hard and towels are soft, challenge them a bit. Say something like, "But they were both cymbals. Shouldn't they both have been loud?"

- What did the towels do to the sound? Children will most often answer by saying that the towels softened the sound. If they do, tell them they're right.

- Does covering hard objects with something soft make them sound softer when they're hit together?

- If you wanted to make other hard instruments, such as rhythm sticks, sound softer, what could you do?

Discovery to Make

Covering hard objects with soft materials will make them sound softer when they're hit together.

IT'S NOT ABOUT THE CYMBALS

It's always fun to bang cymbals together, and it's fun to try new things, such as covering cymbals with towels to find out what they'll sound like. This activity, however, is about learning to reflect on one's own thinking processes. It's also about considering seemingly conflicting information—"They were both cymbals, shouldn't they both be loud?"—and reasoning through it.

WHY DOES SOUND MOVE DIFFERENTLY THROUGH AIR, LIQUID, AND SOLID THINGS?

By this point, the children understand that sound can move through air, liquids, and solids. They've also learned that the same sound will be louder moving through solids than through the air. What they don't know, and what they've probably already asked you many times, is why. How can anything move easily through something as hard as a wooden table? They're about to find out.

What You'll Need

No materials needed

Activity to Try

1. Ask the class whether sound can move through air, liquids, and solids. How do they know? See if they can remember the activities that demonstrated the movement of sound, such as "Can Sound Move through a Solid Object?" and if they can explain those activities.

2. Ask if they've wondered why sound moves through solids louder and faster than it moves through the air. Remind them that we can walk easily through the air, but we can't walk through the wall. How do they think sound can go through solids so easily? Listen to children's answers, and for now, simply acknowledge each response with a nod or a "mm-hm."

3. Explain that you're going to try an activity to show how sound moves through air, liquids, and solids. Ask the children whether they know that air, liquids, and solids—in fact, everything in the whole world—is made up of tiny little things called molecules. You could bring out one grain of sand from the sand table and bring it around the circle for each child to see. Tell them that molecules are much, much smaller than that! Some children may have heard the word molecule and will want to tell the class about it, which is great. Children often listen more attentively to their peers' explanations than to teachers'.

4. Tell the class that sound is a kind of movement, but for us to hear it, it has to bump into molecules, which bump into other molecules and keep the sound moving along. Explain that in the air, molecules are very far apart, so it takes quite a while for sound to bump into one molecule and have that one bump into another. In liquids, the molecules are closer together, and it takes less time for sound to move from molecule to molecule. In solids, molecules are packed in very tightly together, so the vibration of sound goes very fast from molecule to molecule. Tell the children you're going to act this out, by pretending to be molecules!

5. Ask about a third of the group to be air molecules. (Other children should remain seated.) The "air molecules" should stand in the middle of the circle, as far away from each other as they can. Explain that you're going to start the vibration by bumping the side of your arm gently into the arm of one of the "air molecules." Then they'll keep the vibration going by gently bumping another molecule, and so on, until they've all been bumped. Be sure the children understand what to do.

6. Act out the same demonstration with a group of "liquid molecules" standing a little more than a foot apart.

7. Act out the demonstration with "solid molecules" packed very closely together. Sometimes I tell them, "Molecules don't fall on the floor," which is not always true, but it helps them remember to be gentle.

8. Make sure that each child is included in one of the molecule groups.

Questions to Ask

- Who can tell me what a molecule is?

- Are air molecules close together or far apart? How about liquid molecules? Solid molecules?

- How did sound move through the air, liquid, and solid molecules?

- Why is it easier for sound to move through solids than through the air?

Discoveries to Make

- Everything in the world is made up of tiny things called molecules.

- Air molecules are far apart. Liquid molecules are closer together. Solid molecules are very close together.

- Sound moves through solids more easily than through the air because the molecules of a solid are so close together. It takes less time in solids for sound to bump into one molecule and have that molecule bump the next one.

TIP

Young children have a lot of fun with this activity, but the concepts aren't simple. Take your time, and make sure each step is understood before you move on to the next. Also, once they've been through the whole activity, everybody will want to be a "solid molecule" and experience all the fast bumping. If you think your group can handle it without getting too silly, let them all be solid molecules and bunch close together. Start the sound by bumping one of them, and watch some very giggly molecules!

The molecule-bumping fun from the "Why Does Sound Move Differently through Air, Liquid, and Solid Things?" activity continues with this singing game. As the children change from air molecules to liquid molecules to solid molecules, they can understand in a concrete, tactile way how sound moves through each medium. This reinforces their understanding in a playful, informal context, and all the molecules have a great time.

What You'll Need

A very large space, such as a playground area

Activity to Try

1. Tell the class that you're going to play a game about sound moving through molecules of air, liquid, and solids. Ask whether anyone remembers if air molecules are close together or far apart. Children will remember that they're far away from each other.

2. Have the group form a circle, with each child standing two or three feet apart from the children on either side. They shouldn't be moving yet. Tell them that when you start to sing and bump into someone to start the sound vibration moving, then they'll make the bump keep going from one person to the next. Remind them to bump gently.

3. Sing to the tune of the "Dinah, won't you blow" section of "I've Been Working on the Railroad":

> *Moving through the air,* (children bump into each other)
>
> *Moving through the air,*
>
> *Sound is moving through the air.*
>
> *Moving through the air,*
>
> *Moving through the air,*
>
> *Sound is moving through the air!*

4. Repeat, with children standing a bit closer. Sing "Moving through the liquid . . ." a little faster than the previous verse.

5. Have children stand very close together and bump along quickly, for "Moving through a solid . . . ," which you can sing at a fast pace. Remind the children to bump carefully.

6. If the class would like to, you can continue the game, mixing up the order of air, liquid, and solid to add to the silly fun.

Questions to Ask

- How does sound move through the air—quickly or slowly?
- When it moves through liquid, does sound go slower or faster than through the air?
- What's the fastest way for sound to move?
- Why does sound move differently through air, liquid, and solids? It may be hard for them to articulate the reason in detail. Children should be able to express the general concept that sound moves more easily when molecules are close together than when they're farther apart. When all the children understand, you can talk about the fact that sound carries energy through the molecules. Sound gives the molecules the energy to bump into each other.

> **TIP**
>
> Children can play this singing game indoors by using blocks, cars, or toy dinosaurs to pretend to be the molecules.

Discoveries to Make

- Sound moves through different materials in different ways.
- Sound carries energy through molecules of different materials.

CHAPTER THREE

DIFFERENT OBJECTS, DIFFERENT SOUNDS: THE SCIENCE OF TIMBRE, OR SOUND QUALITY

Here's a way to get students thinking about differences in sound. Have two rhythm instruments in a large shopping bag so the children can't see them. The two instruments should be familiar to all the children and have very distinctive sounds—say, a triangle and a shaker. Tell the group that you're going to play the instruments in the bag, and they should listen carefully but not say anything yet. Play the triangle and then the shaker, without removing them from the bag. (For uniformity's sake, strike or shake each instrument three times.)

KEY CONCEPT

Different objects and materials make different sounds.

Then ask the class whether you played the same instrument twice or played two different instruments. Of course, they'll know the instruments were different and will probably be able to tell you which instruments they were, too. Ask them, "How did you know they were different instruments?"

Some may answer, "Because they sounded different," or "Our ears could tell the sounds were different." This will lead you to ask, "Can you tell me how the instruments sounded different?"

You'll hear things like, "One was loud and one was softer," "One made a *ding!* kind of sound," "The second one sounded shaky," and so on, plus more imaginative replies, such as "One sounded like a clock," or "One sounded like when you're pouring cereal." Accept all responses without judgment; every answer shows that they're thinking. You can even say, "I can tell you're doing a lot of thinking! That's great."

Now it's time for the big reveal: Take the triangle and the shaker out of the bag. The children were right!

Then ask them if they've ever wondered why different things sound different. Tell them that they're going to be learning about this. Meanwhile, ask them to be thinking about questions, such as Why do musical instruments sound different from each other? Why does your mom's voice sound different from yours? Does every object have its own kind of sound? Tell them that soon you'll all find out together about how and why different things make different sounds.

DIFFERENT KINDS OF DRUMS

The drum was one of the first musical instruments used by humans. It's also one of the first instruments most young children play. So, by the time they're in preschool, children are very familiar with drums and confident in their ability to play them. That's why I like to start with drums in our activities exploring sound quality. With no explanations or instructions needed, students can delve into their scientific exploration right away.

What You'll Need

Drums, including empty coffee cans with lids

Large bag

Dry-erase easel or large paper and marker

Activity to Try

1. Have the drums in a closed bag next to you. Ask the children to sit in a circle. Tell the group that you'll be trying out different kinds of drums, and you'll talk about the ways the drums sound the same and the ways they sound different.

2. Take the drums out from the bag one at a time, and put them in front of you. The easiest way to set up the exploring is simply to hand a drum to the child on your right. Invite him to play it for a few moments, trying different ways to play it and focusing on the sounds he hears. Then he can pass it to the child on his right and choose another drum to try.

3. Continue until each child has had a turn with each drum. Encourage the children to talk quietly so those playing drums can hear the sounds clearly.

4. As an alternative, you could have the children play with the drums at a "drumming center" for a week or so. This allows for more time for students to play and explore. On the other hand, it's harder for you to make sure that each child has tried every drum.

Questions to Ask

- Hold up each drum, and ask the group to describe what it sounded like.
- Did it make a short, flat sound or did its sound continue for a bit after you hit it? This is called resonating.
- Did the drum's sound remind you of something else you've heard? Some of their answers will be "unscientific," such as, "That one sounded like it came from the jungle." That's fine. They're distinguishing between the sounds, and that's the important thing.
- How did the drums sound the same? Children might say they all sounded like someone hitting something, they all sounded loud, or they all sounded like *boom* or *thunk* or another descriptive word.
- Review the children's observations with a T-chart. Let them tell you which descriptive words and phrases to write. It may look something like this:

HOW DRUMS WERE THE SAME	HOW DRUMS WERE DIFFERENT
had a thumpy sound	some were loud, some were softer
all were hit with a hand	some sounded higher, some lower
they were all round	some were bigger, some were smaller

- Did all of the drums sound the same, or did each one sound different? Tell them that every instrument has its own special sound. This is called its sound quality, or *timbre* (pronounced "tamber").

Discovery to Make

Each kind of instrument has its own unique sound, called its *timbre*.

Just for fun, you can tell the children that humans aren't the only animals to play drums. Scientists have found that monkeys and chimpanzees also play rhythmically on "drums" of fallen logs and other objects (Remedios, Logothetis, and Kayser, 2013).

MALLETS AND BRUSHES

In the "Different Kinds of Drums" activity, children used only their hands to play each instrument. This was for a reason. It established that the differences in timbre they heard were coming only from the materials and structures of the instruments themselves.

Now you're going to add some new variables—some really fun variables! Bring in all sorts of mallets and brushes—both traditional and otherwise—and let the children experiment with them. They will find out whether they can use these tools to change the timbre of the drums.

What You'll Need

1 kind of drum or drum-like object for every two children

Variety of mallets and brushes, such as wooden or rubber-tipped mallets, plastic or metal spoons, unsharpened pencils, clean pastry or basting brushes, large clean paint brushes, or clean toothbrushes

Large bag

Recording of music with a steady beat (see "Suggested Recordings of Instrumental Music" on page 190)

Activity to Try

1. Have drums, mallets, and brushes in a closed bag next to you. You will need a mallet or brush for each child. Tip: You can make interesting-sounding mallets by wrapping rubber bands around the top of an unsharpened pencil, and then covering the top in soft fabric, held in place with another rubber band. Note: Do not use real drumsticks, rhythm sticks, or other long, heavy sticks for this activity—overenthusiastic musicians can cause accidents with these.

2. Bring out a drum and a mallet. Bang on the drum a few times with the mallet, and ask the class if they know what it (the mallet) is called. Tell them it's a *mallet*.

3. Ask the children why they think people use mallets on drums. After you've heard the children's ideas, tell them you're going to explore mallets and other things to hit drums with, and you'll find out if they make the drums have different sounds, or timbres.

4. Set out the drums in a row down the center of the circle. Then, set two different mallets or brushes, one on either side, for each drum.

5. Have one child sit by each mallet or brush, but ask her not to play yet.

6. Explain the activity. Tell the children you're going to put on some background music. When the music starts, children on one side should start to play. You'll stop the music after a while to give the other side a turn. Ask the children to listen carefully to the sounds made by the mallets and brushes.

7. Start the music, not too loudly, and begin the activity.

8. Afterward, have each pair of partners explain to the group what their mallets or brushes sounded like, and whether the sounds were the same or different.

TIP

Chances are that many children will want to try out all the mallets and brushes. If possible, bring them out with the drums later in the day for free play, with teacher supervision.

Questions to Ask

- Why do you think the timbre each mallet or brush produced was different?
- Why do you think using mallets sounds different from using your hands to play?
- What about the brushes? How did they make the drums sound?
- Does playing a drum with different mallets or brushes change the timbre of the drum?

Discovery to Make

Children can change the timbre of a drum by hitting it with different mallets or brushes.

·ı|ı|ı WHISTLES, RECORDERS, AND OTHER WIND INSTRUMENTS ||ı|ı·

Anthropologists have found many wind instruments made from animal bones dating as far back as 33,000 BC. Since they seem carefully crafted and produce a variety of tones, scientists speculate they were used purposefully for social bonding and as part of sacred rituals.

I always feel conflicted when I present activities with these instruments, because I can't let all the children try them out, for obvious hygienic reasons. However, wind instruments are a basic part of the musical instrument family—and a beautiful part. Even if children can only listen to them, they are well worth studying for their unique sounds.

What You'll Need

Variety of wind instruments, such as a metal whistle, a recorder, a plastic toy flute, a tin flute, a plastic whistle, a pan flute, an ocarina, a harmonica, a wooden train whistle, and a real flute

Large bag

Activity to Try

1. Have the instruments in a closed bag next to you. Introduce this exploration by turning away from the children, taking a metal whistle out of the bag, and blowing into it. That gets their attention! Almost immediately, they'll ask if they can play it. You'll need to explain that because your mouth has been on it, the instrument carries your germs and wouldn't be okay to share.

2. Tell the children that a whistle is one of many instruments called *wind instruments* because people blow their breath through them, like the wind blows. Add that you'll be playing several different kinds of wind instruments and the children should listen carefully to the different sounds, or timbres, made by each one.

3. Pick up the recorder and play a short, familiar song, such as "Twinkle, Twinkle, Little Star." The students will be excited to hear a tune they recognize and will often shout out the name of the song. Tell them they're right, and tell them the instrument is called a recorder. Ask them if they can guess how you played different notes. Many will have noticed how you covered and uncovered the holes with your fingertips.

4. Play the other instruments, ending with the train whistle and the harmonica.

5. Add that some people can whistle through their lips. If you can, demonstrate it. If not, ask if any of the children can whistle. They'll be happy to show you, and the other children will be eagerly trying to whistle for the rest of the day!

Questions to Ask

- Why do you think the whistles sounded so loud when I blew into them? Basically, it's because a lot of air—the breath you blew into it—was squeezed through a tiny space, creating many fast vibrations as the air bounced around in that small space.

- Why do you think I was able to play a lot of different notes with the recorder, but not with the whistle?

- Children usually realize it has something to do with the holes. You can show them how covering different combinations of holes produces different tones.

- What about the train whistle and the harmonica? Did they sound different from the other instruments, or about the same? You can explain that a train whistle actually has four tubes inside it, so each time you blow into it, you produce four tones at the same time. A harmonica has ten holes, and you can cover more than one hole at a time with your mouth. Also, there are metal parts inside each hole that make the air vibrate in even more ways. That's why we hear so many sounds. The instruments have different structures—they're built differently. You can go around the circle and show each child the four holes in the mouth of the train whistle and the ten holes of the harmonica.

- If I just blow like this (blow out with your mouth into the air), you don't hear a musical tone. Why does blowing into a whistle or through squished-together lips produce such a loud tone?

> **TIP**
>
> While reminding children not to put their mouths on the instruments, you can give them time to examine the various instruments, to see what they're made of and how they're constructed. Stay with them while they do this and be available to discuss their observations.

Exploring the Science of Sounds: 100 Musical Activities for Young Children

Discoveries to Make

- Whistles and other wind instruments (including our own whistling) work by squeezing the air we blow through a very small space, which makes the air vibrate very fast, creating a sharp, high-pitched timbre.

- The structures of the instruments affect their sounds. (Structure and function is a crosscutting concept that applies to every domain of science.)

DIFFERENT KINDS OF STRINGED INSTRUMENTS

Children are absolutely enchanted by the sound of a guitar. Whenever I bring out a guitar or ukulele, their faces lean in with utter fascination. Many young children have heard family members or friends play guitars and are very excited to find out more about stringed instruments.

What You'll Need

Large, thick rubber band

Tuning fork

Assortment of stringed instruments, such as a guitar, a ukulele, a violin, or a banjo

Activity to Try

1. Tell the children that you're going to be exploring how stringed instruments produce sound. Bring out the plain rubber band. Stretch it with one hand and pluck it with the index finger of your other hand. Ask if everyone could hear the sound. They may need to come closer. Ask if the sound was loud or soft.

2. Strum one or two of the instruments, so the children can hear the sounds. If you can, play a song or two on one of the instruments.

3. Take each instrument around the circle for children to strum or pluck, with your supervision.

Questions to Ask

- How does a guitar or ukulele produce sounds? After listening to responses, explain that plucking or strumming the guitar's strings starts a vibration. The vibration goes into the bridge—the part at the lower end of the strings that holds the strings above the surface of the instrument—and then moves through the wood. Most of the sound we hear comes from the wood vibrating. Some sound is also vibrating inside the guitar—this sound comes out through the sound hole.

- Do you think a guitar would sound the same if we covered the sound hole? After they discuss this, try it out! Hold a piece of cardboard over the sound hole while you strum or pluck the strings.
- Why do stringed instruments have wooden bodies? Sound travels more easily through solids, so the wood makes the sound louder.

Discovery to Make

Stringed instruments have wooden bodies to make the sound louder, because sound travels more easily through solids. Also, the sound vibrating inside the body makes even more sound. This relates to the crosscutting concepts of structure and function.

KEEP THE LEARNING GOING!

During free play, bring out a ukulele or guitar. Let the children experiment with different ways to strum and pluck the strings, with your supervision.

DANCING WITH PAPER

I'm not a hoarder, but I do have an extensive collection of musical materials most people would probably consider garbage. Boxes, bags, wrappers, packaging material—if it makes an interesting sound when I tap, crumple, rip, or shake it, it goes into my bag—okay, several bags—of potential music. Fortunately, young children are a lot like me in this respect. Where grown-ups see junk, they see musical instruments, construction materials, or dramatic props. Where adults see weeds, they see flowers. Their world still has unlimited possibilities. We're going to explore some of those possibilities in this activity.

What You'll Need

Variety of paper—scrap paper, notebook paper, newspaper, waxed paper, and so on in a variety of sizes

Large bag

Recording of instrumental music (see "Suggested Recordings of Instrumental Music" on page 190)

Activity to Try

1. Have all your various paper types in a bag next to you. Tell the children that you're going to be doing something they've probably never done before. Tell them you're going to dance with paper.

2. Have the group stand up. Before you hand out the paper, take out a piece and show them a few ways to dance with it. For example, you could shake it while holding it with both hands, rustle it gently, flap it firmly, wave it from side to side, and move it with one hand and then the other. This isn't meant to show them how to dance, but rather to demonstrate that there's no one right way to do it.

3. Pass out the pieces of paper in such a way that there's a good mix of paper types. Ask the children to listen to the paper and observe what it sounds like as they do different movements with it.

4. Start the music, not too loud, and do the Paper Dance!

5. Continue for about a minute, pause, and have the children trade so they have a different kind of paper. Dance again, then have another switch after a while.

6. When the musical selection is over, have the children sit down again. Collect the paper sheets. Children should wash their hands after this activity. The newspaper will leave some ink on their hands.

> **TIP**
>
> As you're dancing with the class, notice their movements. Acknowledge with an excited smile or a silent "Wow!" when a child tries a move you haven't seen or thought of before. Share their enthusiasm as they try new ways to make different sounds with these interesting materials. This helps children develop self-confidence and creative-thinking skills.

Questions to Ask

- What was it like to dance with the paper?
- Which kind of paper did you find to be the loudest? Which was the quietest? Why do you think that was?
- Did it make a difference how you moved the paper? Was one way of moving it particularly loud?
- How did the paper make sound?
- How do you think we could make an even louder sound with paper? If they say "Use heavier paper," "Use more sheets at a time," or "Use bigger sheets of paper," try those ideas out, today or another time. Try heavy paper, such as art paper used for sketching, and large pieces of paper, such as full sheets of newspaper. Find out if their ideas work.

Discoveries to Make

- Shaking or flapping paper makes sound by creating a vibration that moves through the air.
- Using larger pieces of paper, or heavier paper, produces more sound when shaken than lighter, smaller pieces.

LET'S CRUMPLE!

Whenever I design activities, whether they're focused on creative thinking or reasoning skills, I try to base them on my observations of what young children do "in the wild" when they're on their own. I've observed that they like to crumple things up: papers they're done with, snack wrappers, dirty paper bags. If it can be crumpled, it will be crumpled. It just seems more satisfying for them to throw something away if they've crumpled and crushed and generally destroyed it first. Crumpling is a sound worth exploring since it's so distinctive. For this activity, children can crumple paper to their hearts' content—and learn something, too.

What You'll Need

Plenty of paper, such as notebook or copy paper, magazine paper, and waxed paper

Large bag

Activity to Try

1. Hold a piece of plain notebook or copy paper so all the children can see it. Tell them that you're going to put the paper in the bag, and then do something to it. Ask them to listen closely to try to figure out what you're doing.

2. Put the paper in the bag, and crumple it as loudly as you can. Most children will know right away that you were crumpling it up. Congratulate them on their excellent listening.

3. Explain that you're going to crumple different kinds of paper. Tell them they will find out what kinds of sounds each type of paper makes when they crumple it.

4. Give each child a sheet of notebook or copy paper, but tell them not to crumple it yet. Remind them not to talk while they're crumpling, because you want everyone to be able to hear the sound.

5. When everyone has paper, say, "One, two, three—crumple!" so they'll all crumple their papers at the same time. This isn't just for fun—it magnifies the crumpling sound so children can hear it easily.

6. Repeat the process with the magazine paper and the waxed paper. Everyone should wash their hands afterward—the magazine paper will leave some ink on their hands.

Questions to Ask

- Which paper sounded the loudest? Which sounded the softest?

- How would you describe the sound made when you crumpled the waxed paper? Children might just reply "loud," but some will use more descriptive words like "crackly" or "crispy."

- Did crumpling the paper sound different from shaking the paper, or did it sound the same? If it sounded different, how was it different? Why do think it sounded different? If the children aren't sure, demonstrate shaking paper and then crumpling the same piece, for them to compare.

Just for fun, since you have all those crumpled-up balls of paper, play a game! Let the children take turns tossing a crumple-ball at a chair across the room to see if they can hit the seat of the chair.

Discovery to Make

Paper has different timbres depending on what kind of movement is done with it.

 WATER AND ICE

Even young children have heard the sounds of water for years. They've heard it pour from faucets and pitchers; they've heard it splash in a pool or at the beach. They may think they know all about the sounds of water, but water has another trick up its sleeve. It can change! Will it still sound the same? Stay tuned.

What You'll Need

2 opaque containers, such as travel coffee mugs with lids

Water

Cup of ice cubes

Activity to Try

1. Out of sight of the children, fill one of the containers half-full with water and put the lid on. Leave the other one empty.

2. Have the container with water in front of you. Wonder aloud about what's in it. Pick it up, hold it next to your ear, and gently shake it. Look surprised at the sound. The children will hear something sloshing inside the container and call out things like, "It's coffee!" or "Water! It's water in there!" If they do, you could ask them how they know and why they think so. Get them thinking. Ask if it could be milk or juice or something else.

3. Pass the container around the circle for children to gently shake and listen to closely. Remind them not to open the container.

4. Ask them if they're still sure it's coffee or water, or if they think it could be something else. Get a show of hands—how many children think that because you can't see inside, you can't say for sure what it is?

5. Open the container and pour it into a clear glass. Confirm that they didn't know that until they saw it.

6. Ask the children if there's any way you could make the water make a louder, harder, bumpy sound. If they're not sure, model a reasoning process. Say something like, "Well, let's think about things that we know make loud, hard, and bumpy sounds. What are some of those things?" Listen to all responses. Children usually say rocks, beads, blocks, and other toys.

7. Ask the children if all those things are a gas like air, a liquid like water, or a solid like a table. They'll know those items are solids. Ask them if water is a solid. They'll remember it's a liquid. Ask them if there's any way to turn water into a solid.

8. At this point, many children will remember that water turns into ice when it's frozen. If not, continue to lead them with questions, such as "What happens to a lake or pond in winter, so that people can skate on it?"

9. When all the children agree that freezing the water into ice cubes will make it sound loud, hard, and bumpy, tell them you need to try it out to see if they're right.

10. Have another teacher bring you the cup of ice cubes. Let the class watch as you put some ice cubes into the empty container and replace the lid.

11. Pass the container around the circle for children to shake and listen to.

Questions to Ask

- What did the water sound like at first? What kind of noises did it make?
- What did the ice sound like?
- Ice is just water that's frozen. Why is the sound so much louder and bumpier when the water turns into ice?

Discoveries to Make

- Water in a shaken container sounds different from ice in a shaken container.
- Water changes from a liquid to a solid when it's frozen. This relates to energy and matter, crosscutting concepts that apply to all domains of science. In this case, children learn about liquids and solids, two of the three states of matter.

> **KEEP THE LEARNING GOING!**
>
> It's interesting to pour some of the ice into the container of water. Have children predict what it will sound like if they shake it. Let them try it and find out!

THE SKATER'S WALTZ

Paper plates aren't just for picnics. Today they're staying indoors so you can investigate the sounds they produce when you tap them, clap them, flap them, and even skate on them!

What You'll Need

Paper plates, two for each child

Skating music—anything slow and smooth will do. I like "The Skater's Waltz" by Émile Waldteufel.

Activity to Try

1. Hold up two paper plates. Suggest that you could make different sounds with paper plates.
2. Give each child two plates, but ask them not to play yet. Ask the children for ideas: How could we use the plates to make sounds? Children may suggest clapping them together. Have everyone try it, and ask them to describe the sound.

3. Do the same for other suggestions—possibly flapping or flying them in the air, tapping them on knees, and so on. Try out the ideas and ask the children to describe the sounds produced.

4. Tell the children you're going to do something a little different. Stand up (asking children to stay seated), and step on your plates, which should be lying right side up. Tell the class you're going to pretend the circle is a frozen pond. Ask if they think you could skate across the pond on the paper plates. After their answer, "skate" across, modeling a gentle, careful glide.

5. Tell the children that you brought in some special skating music for them and they'll each get a turn to skate. Start the music and let each child take a turn. Remind them to be slow and careful, just like they would be if they were skating on real ice.

6. Collect the paper plates.

Questions to Ask

- We did a lot of things with the paper plates. Did the plates always sound the same?
- What were some of the different sounds we made?
- How do you think it was possible for the paper plates to make all those different sounds?

Discovery to Make

Some objects can make different sounds, depending on how we use them.

> ### KEEP THE LEARNING GOING!
>
> For an extra challenge, have children skate in pairs, holding hands. This requires cooperation and coordination. Children could also try to skate on different kinds of plates, such as heavy cardboard or plastic.

ALUMINUM FOIL SOUNDS

You couldn't invent a material that is more fascinating to young children than aluminum foil. It's as light as paper, yet looks and feels totally different. It holds its shape when you bend it. It's pliable enough to manipulate easily, and it's dazzlingly shiny. With aluminum foil you can be a robot or a knight. You can create jewelry and fabulous sculptures. Aluminum foil can be used to make all kinds of amazing art projects. Best of all are the exciting, dramatic sounds you can produce with this unique material.

What You'll Need

75-foot roll of regular-size aluminum foil

Sheet of copy paper

Large bag

Activity to Try

1. Have the foil and paper ready in a closed bag. Tell the children that you'll be exploring an amazing material. You can say that it's thin like paper, but comes in a long roll. It's very shiny, and you can bend it in all kinds of ways. You can wrap food in it. By now, some children will have guessed—it's aluminum foil!

2. Bring it out and tear off a sheet about one foot long. Explain to the children that they may not handle the foil box by themselves since it has a very sharp edge. Lay the foil sheet on the floor in front of you.

3. Take out the regular paper and shake it while holding it with both hands. Ask them what they predict the foil will sound like when they shake it in the same way.

4. Tear off a sheet of foil for each child. Lay one sheet of foil in front of each student, but tell them not to touch it yet. When everyone has foil, let them pick it up and shake it.

5. Show the group how to fold the sheet of foil in half, flatten it out, then fold it again. They can then shake the folded sheet, noting how it sounds.

6. After they've shaken it for a while, have them crumple the foil slowly, right next to their ears.

Questions to Ask

- Did shaking the sheet of foil sound the same or different from shaking paper?
- If it sounded different, how did it sound different? Can you describe the timbre of the foil?
- What did crumpling the foil sound like?
- What happened to the sound after you folded the foil?
- Why do you think foil sounds different from paper when you shake it?

Discoveries to Make

- Foil sounds different from paper when it's shaken because it's made of metal.
- Things made of metal sound different from things made of paper.

KEEP THE LEARNING GOING!

Ask the children to tell you about other things they know that are made of metal.

ㅏㅣㅣㅣㅣ PLASTIC AND METAL SPOONS ㅣㅣㅣㅣㅣ

The objectives of this short activity are to build children's confidence in their ability to predict results and to further familiarize them with the basics of scientific explorations and thinking—asking a question, predicting the answer, experimenting, observing the results, and drawing a conclusion based on the results.

Why are you dancing again in this experiment? Because it helps children think on their feet!

I'm only half joking. There's evidence that young children may learn better when their bodies are in motion (Mullender-Wijnsma et al., 2015). So, I try to include lots of activities where children aren't just sitting. Also, dancing makes it easier for children to use instruments (or in this case, spoons) in a more rhythmic way, playing to the beat of the music.

We're exploring the sounds of plastic and metal again, but this time in a more musical context. Many musical instruments—both children's instruments like triangles and jingle bells, and orchestral ones such as trumpets and horns—take advantage of metal's bright, sharp timbre. Even with humble metal spoons, children can enjoy the special sound quality of metal.

What You'll Need

Plastic spoons, two each for half the number of students

Metal spoons, two each for half the number of students

Recording of instrumental music (see "Suggested Recordings of Instrumental Music" on page 190)

Activity to Try

1. Tell the children that you'll be doing an experiment where you dance with spoons! Show the class the two kinds of spoons they'll be playing—plastic and metal. Tell them you brought some fun music for them to dance to while they play.

2. Remind them that every experiment starts with a question. Tell them that the question is, "Which will sound louder when you hit them together, plastic spoons or metal spoons? Or will they sound the same?" You may hear some excited shouts right away—"Metal! Metal!" Or the class may reach a consensus on this after some discussion. Remember to ask the children their reasons for making this prediction, but you don't have to make every child state their case. You can just have one or two express their reasons and ask the class if they agree.

3. Confirm that their prediction, or hypothesis, is that the metal spoons will sound louder. Tell them they need to design their experiment to find out if they're right. Ask them how they can find out which spoons are louder. At least some of the children will know that they need to play both kinds of spoons, listen, and compare the sounds.

4. Before you pass out the spoons, demonstrate with "air spoons" that they can play the spoons any way they like—high in the air or down low, loud or soft, fast or slow, on top of each other, clicking side to side. They should just be careful to stay in their spot and respect the space of the people around them.

5. Pass out pairs of spoons to the students, alternating between plastic and metal pairs.

6. Put on the music, dance, and play! In the middle of the recording, pause and have everyone trade with their neighbor so they can play the other kind of spoons.

TIP

Playing spoons has been a musical tradition for centuries, especially in Irish, Central Asian, and French-Canadian folk music. I really like this video, with a very talented young man, unfortunately uncredited, playing with an Irish folk band: https://www.youtube.com/watch?v=8SY6JLwdz5c. Your students will be amazed to hear what spoons can sound like!

Questions to Ask

- What did the plastic spoons sound like?
- What did the metal spoons sound like?
- Which kind of spoons were louder?
- Was your hypothesis right?
- Why do you think the metal spoons were louder?

Discoveries to Make

- Metal spoons struck together made a louder sound than plastic spoons.
- Children can design experiments to test their hypotheses and answer questions.
- When objects are the same size, those made of metal may be louder than those made of plastic.

THE TOP AND BOTTOM OF A COFFEE CAN

Coffee can drums may not be fancy, but they're excellent musical instruments for young children. They sound enjoyably solid and thumpy but not overly loud. They're easy for small hands to manipulate, and they're remarkably durable. What I love most about coffee cans is the fact that they're two sounds in one. Because the lid is plastic and the bottom and sides are metal, coffee cans have two separate timbres for children to play and hear.

What You'll Need

Metal coffee cans with plastic lids, one for each child

Large bag

Activity to Try

1. Have the coffee cans in a closed bag next to you. Bring out one can. Ask the class what it is.

2. Ask the children what they think it's made of. They might not know, since the shiny metal is covered with colored paper or is painted. If they're not sure, prompt them with some possibilities: Could it be wood, or glass, or paper? If they can't guess, tell them they may be able to tell what it's made of when they play it.

3. Take off the lid and show it to the class. Ask what they think the lid is made of. This is also a good opportunity to show them that the can is empty, because if you don't show them, many children will take off the lid as soon as they have the can in their hands. The curiosity is admirable, but it's often difficult for them to replace the lid securely, and the experiment will be interrupted while you help replace several lids.

4. Tell the children they'll be doing an experiment to answer a question: Which will sound louder when you hit it—the top (the lid) or the bottom? (Show the group the bottom of the can.) Or will they sound the same?

5. Ask for a show of hands. Count the predictions for "The top," those for "The bottom," and those for "They'll both sound the same." Ask if anyone can explain why they think their prediction is right. If no one refers to it, ask them if they remember the "Which Will Sound Louder, Rhythm Sticks Hitting a Hard Floor or Mittens Hitting a Hard Floor?" activity. Ask what they found out in that experiment.

6. Pass out the cans, but ask the children not to play them yet.

7. Have them hit the top of the can a few times and then hit the bottom a few times. Remind the class not to shout out answers yet—let's give everyone a chance to experiment and listen.

Questions to Ask

- Which was louder, the top or the bottom? Listen to one child's answer, and ask the students to raise their hands if they agree.
- Did the bottom of the can sound just louder than the top, or did it also sound different?
- Why did the bottom sound louder than the top? Some students may say it's because the bottom of the can is harder than the top. That's true—that's why the bottom is louder. If they didn't know before, ask whether anyone can say now what the top and bottom are made of.

Discoveries to Make

- Hard things make louder sounds than soft things when we hit them.
- The top, or lid, of a coffee can is made of soft plastic, and the bottom is made of metal.

> **KEEP THE LEARNING GOING!**
>
> Some children may be curious about the sides of the can, wondering what the metal is covered with and what it looks like underneath. If the cans are covered in paper, help them to remove the coverings. They can discover the metal underneath. Do they see how the paper was attached to the metal? This may seem basic to us, but many children like nothing more than taking things apart to see what's inside—a very scientific enterprise that is generally off limits to young children.

ADDING THUNDER TO A STORY ABOUT A STORM

Obviously, this activity reinforces the idea that metal materials have a bright, piercing sound quality. But I like this game for another reason. Whenever I put aluminum foil in the same room with young children, at some point there's going to be a "storm." Children love to pretend to scare each other (and themselves) with "lightning" and "thunder" they create by shaking long pieces of foil. (To me, shaking foil sounds more like rain falling, but they always like to pretend it's thunder and lightning.) Thunderstorms are exciting and often frightening events for them, and being in control of their own storm helps them express these feelings.

What You'll Need

75-foot roll of regular-size aluminum foil

Sound-making items such as copy paper, newspaper, waxed paper, rhythm sticks, and coffee cans

Picture book about a storm, such as *Creak! Said the Bed* by Phyllis Root, *Drip, Drop* by Sarah Weeks, *Storm Is Coming!* by Heather Tekavec, and *The Big Storm: A Very Soggy Counting Book* by Nancy Tafuri

Activity to Try

1. This is a two-day activity. On the first day, display the aluminum foil and the other sound-making items on the floor in the middle of the circle. Explain that you'll be talking about them later.

2. Tell the children that you will read a story about a storm to them. Ask them to think as they listen about sounds they could make, using the aluminum foil and the other materials, to help tell the story when you read it again tomorrow. Explain that they can make sound effects for thunder, lightning, light rain, heavy rain, animal sounds, walking or running sounds, or any other sounds mentioned in the story.

3. Read the story.

4. On the second day, review the story page by page, and ask the children for ideas for materials with timbres that go with the action on each page. Give as many children as possible an opportunity to contribute. This may involve having several children make "thunder" with foil and/ or drums and expanding the story to include audible things that are pictured but not talked about in the story, such as people running.

5. Review the sounds the children will make and the cues for making sounds—for example, when you read the words *pitter-patter*, they could lightly tap their fingertips on the drums. Let them choose their materials for sound making.

6. Read the story again, with the children making their sound effects.

Questions to Ask

- How did you decide what kind of sound to use for each noise or animal in the story?
- Did the sounds you chose make any difference in how you heard the story? Was it more exciting or less exciting?
- Why does the aluminum foil make that loud, bright sound?
- Did the aluminum foil remind you of the sound of the storm? What if we had used the plain paper? Would that have sounded as exciting? Why not?

Discovery to Make

The bright sound of metal, as well as other sounds, can be used to make stories more exciting.

TRICKS WITH TRIANGLES

My feelings about triangles are complicated. Of course they're wonderful instruments—with one sharp tap of the striker, they produce a clear, pure, and distinctive sound. And how cool is it that it's not just called a triangle, but it's actually in the shape of a triangle? This fact delights young children. I suspect they think it's just an amazing coincidence. Great sound, fun to play, helps teach about shapes—what's not to like?

Triangles are loud! As an early childhood music teacher, I'm used to living in the land of high decibels, but triangles are on a whole other level. They're best in extremely small doses, but this activity takes anywhere from fifteen minutes to half an hour, so consider yourself warned. Even with this drawback, the triangle is a unique instrument that's a lot of fun to play and explore.

What You'll Need

Triangles with metal strikers

Soft material to cover each triangle, such as small towels or baby blankets

Additional objects to use as strikers, such as unsharpened pencils or craft sticks

Tuning fork

Large bag

Activity to Try

1. Bring out a triangle. Keep the other objects in a closed bag. Tell the class that they'll be doing a lot of tricks with the triangle.
2. Hold the triangle by the loop, and ask a nearby child to strike it with the striker. *Ding!* The familiar sound will ring out. Ask the children what they think will happen if you hold one side of the triangle while someone else hits it with the striker? Do they think it will sound the same? Listen to responses.

3. Try it out. You'll hear kind of a hollow *click!,* as if the triangle had suddenly turned into plastic. Ask the children why that happened. Some children will probably guess that holding the triangle stops most of the vibrations, so much less sound can travel through the instrument and the air.

4. Ask the children if they think there's any other way you could change the timbre of the triangle. They may have ideas right away, but if they don't, try reminding them of similar activities they've done, such as "Which Will Sound Louder, Cymbals Crashing into Each Other or Cymbals Wrapped in Small Towels Crashing into Each Other?" How did they make the cymbals sound different? The students will soon be volunteering lots of ideas.

5. Take the other materials out of the bag, and try out the children's suggestions. Include each child in at least one activity, either holding the triangle or hitting it. They can cover the triangle with various materials before hitting it. They can also lay the triangle flat on the floor and hit it. Children can hit the triangle with other items, such as the pencil. They could (carefully) hit it with more than one striker. They may want to see what the sound is like if they hit the triangle in different places—the three sides, the corners, the inside, and the outside. Or children can make a "super triangle" by hooking triangles into each other to make a hanging chain and then striking just the bottom triangle, or all of them.

6. I find that children learn most effectively when they try each technique or see their classmates try each technique, one at a time. When everyone watches and listens to the same thing at the same time, each child reaps the benefits of the entire group's immediate observations.

Questions to Ask

- What happened when we covered the triangle with the towel?
- Was it louder when we laid it flat on the floor? Why not? The floor keeps the triangle from vibrating as much as it does in the air, but the force of the striker isn't strong enough to make the floor vibrate.
- What about when we hit it with other things? Did that change the sound?
- Did it matter where on the triangle we hit it?
- Was the "super triangle" louder than one triangle?
- Does a triangle always sound the same?
- What kinds of things make it sound different?

Discovery to Make

Children can change the sound of a triangle by covering it, laying it on the floor, and hitting it with different objects.

KEEP THE LEARNING GOING!

As children play, walk around with the triangle. Let them experiment with it. They can listen to what happens when they hit the triangle with a plastic building brick, a wooden block, and other toys.

INSIDE THE SHAKER

As I've mentioned before, children often ask me what's inside shakers. In this activity they get a chance to explore the inside. Don't worry. This doesn't involve sacrificing a shaker in the name of science! You're using handmade shakers that have a clear advantage—they're transparent.

What You'll Need

Clear plastic containers, such as peanut butter jars or honey jars

Materials for filling the shakers, such as small jingle bells, wooden and/or plastic beads, paper clips, sand, twist ties, loose plastic tags from bread loaves, cotton puffs, erasers, small pebbles, and so on

Hot-glue gun or duct tape (optional, adult use only)

Large bag

Activity to Try

1. Fill each container halfway with some materials. Make some shakers loud and some softer. If the items inside may be a choking hazard, you can hot-glue the lid to the container or use duct tape to fasten it on securely.

2. Have the shakers in a closed bag beside you. Bring out one of the shakers, and ask the class what they think it will sound like if you shake it, and why. A typical response might be, "I think it'll be quiet because cotton puffs are soft." If, as in this answer, their reasoning is valid, tell them that was good thinking. If their answer doesn't make sense, challenge them gently by saying something like, "Hmm. I'm wondering if it will be loud. When you squeeze a cotton puff, is it hard or soft?" Other children may join in to offer their opinions. Always remind children to be respectful of their classmates even when they disagree with them.

3. Shake the shaker and ask the group about how it sounded. Then pass the shaker, and the others from the bag, around the circle for everyone to shake.

4. After the activity, you can bring out the shakers during free-play time. Children can explore the timbres further, with your supervision.

Questions to Ask

- Which shaker was the loudest? Why?
- Which was the softest? Why?

- Did the shakers make sounds by themselves? What caused them to make a sound? When you shake the shaker with your arm, it causes the "filling" inside to move around and hit the inside of the shaker, making the sound. Everything that happens—every effect—has a cause, something that made it happen.
- Did all the shakers sound the same?
- Why did they all sound different?

Discoveries to Make

- Not all shakers sound the same, and the material inside the shaker affects the timbre.
- The crosscutting concept of cause and effect.
- Hard materials make a louder sound when shaken than soft materials.

KEEP THE LEARNING GOING!

Many opportunities present themselves during the course of a school day to talk with students about cause and effect. Why is the playground wet? What was the cause? The rain last night caused the wetness. What's the cause of the bruise on your knee? You fell down on the sidewalk. (Uh-oh—now they all want to show you their boo-boos! Sorry about that.)

MAKE MUSIC IN THE KITCHEN: SOUNDS OF METAL

Who knows how many musical careers have started on the kitchen floor? Toddlers have a world of fun thumping on pots and pans and crashing lids together. By age four or five, children may tell you they're too old for these simple pleasures. But then why do their faces light up when they see a room filled with saucepans, soup pots, frying pans, and clinking, clanging lids?

It's not just noisy fun—the kitchen orchestra includes some wonderful sounds. The copper and steel of some of the cookware can produce resonant, clear tones. The varied sizes and shapes of the pots and pans, combined with the many ways they can be tapped and hit, open up infinite possibilities. Curious, creative children will surprise you with their scientific and musical discoveries.

What You'll Need

Variety of metal cookware, including lids

Activity to Try

1. Have the pots, pans, and lids spread out in front of you. Try to include some made of stainless steel and some with copper bottoms. Naturally they should be clean, but it doesn't matter if they're not all sparkling and brand-new.

2. Remind the children not to touch them yet—they'll play with them very soon. Ask if anyone can tell the group what all these things are made of. Listen to responses.

3. Tell the children the items are made of metal. Ask what they think the pots and pans will sound like if you hit them or crash them together. Ask them if they think the items will be loud or soft, and why they think so. Ask if they think all the pots, pans, and lids will have the same timbre.

4. Tell the children they can play each item any way they want, and that they should listen carefully to the sound they make. Start passing each "instrument" (two pot lids to crash together counts as one) around the circle.

5. After one instrument has been played by three or four children, start passing around another one. It may seem like it would be easier to let the children just explore the instruments together, all at once. In my experience, this leads to distracting quarreling about sharing the instruments. There always seems to be one item that's deemed more desirable than the others.

> **TIP**
>
> Explorations like this one are a wonderful opportunity to bring richer, more descriptive vocabulary into your classroom. Words describing metallic sounds include *clanging, clattering, crashing, jingling, jangling, thundering, clear, deep, tinny, bright, tinkling, ringing, piercing, heavy, light, harsh, sweet,* and *strong.*

Questions to Ask

- Which "instrument" did you think was the loudest? Why do you think it was so loud?
- Did you notice that some of the pots or pans were made of different kinds of metal?
- Did the different metals have different sounds?
- What were some of the ways you played the pots and pans? Did playing them in different ways change the sound?
- Why didn't all the pots, pans, and lids sound the same?

Discoveries to Make

- There are different kinds of metal, and they each have a different timbre.
- The way they play each "instrument"—heavily or gently, using different parts of the hand, playing in the air or on the floor, and playing on different parts of the item—changes the resulting sound.

GET TAKEOUT:
SOUNDS OF PLASTIC

We briefly contrasted the sound of plastic with the sound of metal in the "Plastic and Metal Spoons" activity, but today, it's all about plastic. Plastics include a wide range of materials, both thick and thin, pliable and brittle, hard and soft. They can be smooth, sharp, scratchy, and squishy, depending on their chemical composition.

We are so surrounded by plastics that we hardly notice them. Most people would never think about the musical properties of plastic. But children, with their wide-ranging investigative minds, can see and hear things in a fresh and unconventional way. You'll explore the sounds of plastics—including those ubiquitous takeout containers. They may be destined for the recycle bin, but that doesn't mean they can't make some music first!

What You'll Need

Variety of plastic items, ideally two for each child

Recording of music with a steady beat (see "Suggested Recordings of Instrumental Music" on page 190)

Activity to Try

Ahead of Time:

Collect a variety of plastic items. Do not include anything sharp, anything small enough for children to swallow, anything that cracks easily, or anything that has contained medicine (including vitamins), alcohol, peanuts, or tree nuts. You can use any size of containers and lids, including foam containers, such as egg cartons.

With the Children:

1. Have all the plastic items spread out on the floor in front of you. Ask the children not to touch anything yet.

2. Ask them whether anyone knows what these items are made of. Most will know they're plastic. Ask if they know where plastic comes from. Listen to their responses.

3. Explain that plastic is a synthetic material, meaning it was made by people—it's not like metal, wood, or other things that are found in nature. Tell the children that people make plastics by combining other materials together.

4. Ask the children what they think it will sound like if you tap two of these items together. Ask if they think it might sound like metal, or wood, or have a completely different timbre.

5. Explain that you're going to explore the sounds you can make with plastic things. You're going to give each child two items. They can tap them together any way they want, or tap them on different parts of their bodies, or think of completely new ways to play them. They can play behind their backs or on the floor. Suggest that they can use their fingers and fingernails—whatever they feel like. Remind them to observe how the way they play changes the sound.

6. Pass out the items in such a way that no child has the exact same two items as the child next to her. This is so you can pause the music in the middle and have children switch instruments with their neighbors.

7. Start the music and begin playing. Look around and notice children who are trying interesting ways to play—give encouragement with nods and smiles. Remember to pause the music and have children switch instruments after a minute or two.

8. When the music ends, have the children put the instruments down.

> **TIP**
>
> If you notice a child playing in a very original and interesting way, such as using a container to tap a lid, scraping a lid against the side of another lid, or tapping items with his toes, ask him to show his idea to the class after the main activity. This acknowledges the child's creativity and helps the others learn a new way to play. Sometimes I'll say to groups of children, "I love to watch how other people are playing—I learn great ideas that way." When we encourage children to share ideas with each other, everybody wins.

Questions to Ask

- Can anyone show me a way they played that made a very quiet sound? How about a loud sound?

- Can anyone show me a scrapey sound?

- Which instruments were hard and stiff? Which were soft, flexible, and easy to bend?

- Did the stiff and flexible instruments make different sounds?

- Did all the plastic instruments sound the same?

- Did plastic instruments sound the same as metal instruments or different? How?

Discoveries to Make

- Different kinds of plastic items make different sounds.

- Playing the same items in different ways can produce different sounds.

- Plastic items sound different from metal items—plastic sounds are duller and are mostly softer, while metal sounds are more resonant (their sounds last longer), clearer, and are mostly louder.

SOUND SOUP

Today's scientists use a tremendous variety of tools and technologies to discern sounds. They can measure decibel levels, resonance, and pitch. It's even possible to distinguish individual voices on recordings by using machines and software that analyze resonant frequencies of the vocal tract. Still, no technology can replace the powers of a skilled and focused observer. For instance, a forensic voice analyst needs more than technology to identify a voice. She listens carefully to the accent, syntax, and breathing patterns on the recording. Every scientific investigation requires concentration and sharp, finely tuned senses.

Activities such as "Sound Soup" sharpen young children's hearing—and their ability to analyze what they hear.

What You'll Need

Large soup pot

Plastic or wooden serving spoon

3 large ziplock bags

Small metal, wooden, and plastic objects

Blanket

Dish towel

Plastic spoon

Metal teaspoon

Craft stick

Activity to Try

Ahead of Time:

1. Fill one bag with the metal objects, another with the wooden objects, and the third with plastic objects.
2. Put the dish towel in the pot to cover the bottom.
3. Drape the blanket over two chairs to make a curtain behind you. It should be tall enough to hide a sitting, squatting, or kneeling child.

With the Children:

1. Have the three bags, the pot, and the serving spoon next to you. A wood or plastic spoon is best; the sound of metal can make the "soup ingredients" harder to hear.

2. Show the children the pot, and tell them they're going to play a listening game. They're going to listen to three kinds of sounds—metal, wood, and plastic—being stirred in a "sound soup."

3. Shake the three bags to remind the children of each material's timbre.

4. Explain how the game is played: The "stirrer" will go behind the curtain with the pot, the serving spoon, and the three bags. The "listener" will have a plastic spoon, a metal teaspoon, and a craft stick in front of her.

5. Choose a "stirrer" and a "listener." Take the stirrer behind the curtain. Have him point to the bag of objects he wants to use, then help him to quietly put each item from the bag into the dish towel-lined pot. Have him bring the pot out to the front. Remind the children watching the game not to shout out what they think the objects are made of.

6. Carefully remove the dish towel and have the child stir the objects with the serving spoon. The "listener" will report her findings by holding up the plastic spoon if she thinks the objects are plastic, the metal teaspoon for metal, and the craft stick for wood.

7. Ask the group for a show of hands—do they agree with the listener?

8. Let the "stirrer" reveal the contents of the "sound soup."

9. Repeat a few times to give more children turns.

Questions to Ask

- Which kind of "soup" was easiest to identify? Which was hardest?
- What if we put even more objects of each kind in the pot? Would that make it easier to tell what was in the soup?
- If we put in objects of different timbres in the pot, do you think you could tell what the objects were?
- Try this with objects of different timbres.
- How did you know which kinds of objects were in each pot of "soup?"

Discoveries to Make

- Children can identify kinds of objects by listening to their particular timbres, even if they can't see the objects.
- Children can represent findings in nonverbal ways, in this case by holding up different objects.

KEEP THE LEARNING GOING!

Keep the curtain, pot, and spoon available for the rest of the day. Children can play the "sound soup" game on their own by having the "listener" close her eyes, while the "stirrer" puts a toy or two in the pot and stirs it. Then the "listener" can say what she thinks is in the "sound soup."

RIG-A-JIG-JIG

One of the most satisfying aspects of teaching music to young children is the opportunity to pass on some traditional songs and games from children's cultures. This musical game may be American or English in origin and is at least 150 years old. For this activity, I've replaced the line "a pretty friend I chanced to meet" with references to various timbres the children have been exploring. Each child chooses an instrument to play and then, away you go!

What You'll Need

Instruments and sound makers of different timbres, one for each child

Activity to Try

1. Place the instruments and sound makers in the middle of the circle so each can be seen easily.

2. Explain to the children that you're going to play a game about different timbres. Each child will get a turn, and you'll sing a song for that child. When the child hears a kind of timbre mentioned in the song, he should choose an instrument in the middle that has that timbre and play it as he walks around the circle.

3. Give them an example. You could say, for instance:

As Carter was walking down the street, (Ask Carter to stand up, enter the circle, and start walking around inside it.)

Down the street, down the street,

A metal instrument he chanced to meet,

Heigh-ho, heigh-ho, heigh-ho! (Carter chooses a metal instrument and plays it as he walks around the circle. As he walks and plays, the song continues.)

Rig-a-jig-jig and away we go,

Away we go, away we go,

Rig-a-jig-jig and away we go,

Heigh-ho, heigh-ho, heigh-ho! (Carter should stay in the middle while you sing for the next person in the circle.)

4. Play the game, mixing up the timbres randomly. As you play, more and more children will join the musical parade in the middle until the whole class is playing.

5. Afterward, have the children put the instruments down.

Questions to Ask

- How did all the timbres sound together?
- Were there any timbres that stood out as much louder than the others?
- How many different timbres did we play in this game? Can you name them all?

Discoveries to Make

- Children know many different timbres and what they sound like.
- Children can classify instruments by timbre.

KEEP THE LEARNING GOING!

Children may enjoy making a chart with you of all the different timbres in the song and the instruments in each category of timbre.

THE SANDPAPER SOUND

Some people find the sound of scraping sandpaper extremely irritating, like fingernails on a blackboard. I've never had a problem with children, but occasionally teachers will run out of the room when the sand blocks come out! If you have this sensitivity, consider yourself warned: you may want to skip this activity. If you're okay with sandpaper, this activity will be a lot of fun. Children love scraping sandpaper—even with their feet!

What You'll Need

Sand blocks—one pair per child

A few sheets of fine-grit sandpaper

2 pairs of large children's socks

Double-sided tape

Large bag

Recording of music with a steady beat (see "Suggested Recordings of Instrumental Music" on page 190)

Activity to Try

Ahead of Time:

Make sandpaper socks. Use double-sided tape to attach rectangles of sandpaper to the soles of large children's socks. The socks should be large enough to fit over children's shoes. I have found that boy's medium, size twelve to fourteen, works well. The fine-grit type of sandpaper has a more pleasant sound than the coarse grit.

With the Children:

1. Have the sandpaper socks in a closed bag next to you. Pass out the sand blocks.

2. Turn on the music, and have the group scrape the sand blocks to the beat of the music for a minute or two. Or, if you do not have enough sand blocks for every child to have a pair, have the children pass one pair around the circle for each child to have a turn to scrape.

3. Stop the music and ask the children to put down the sand blocks.

4. Collect the sand blocks and ask the children if they know what gives the sand blocks their scrapey sound. Listen to their responses. Children may say, "Sand," which is understandable. Most young children are unfamiliar with sandpaper.

5. Explain that the material on the bottom of the sand blocks is sandpaper, which is used to make wooden things, such as chairs, nice and smooth after they're built. It's scrapey because it has lots of little bits of a mineral called aluminum oxide on it.

6. Tell the children you have a way for them to scrape sandpaper with their feet! Ask them if they think feet would make a louder scraping sound than hands. Listen to their responses.

7. Bring out the sandpaper socks, and hold them up so everyone can see. Choose two children and have them sit in the middle of the circle facing each other.

8. Help them put the socks over their shoes. Start the music again (keep it fairly soft), and have them hold up their feet to scrape against the other child's feet.

9. After ten or fifteen seconds, give another two children a turn. Continue until everyone's had the sandpaper-socks experience.

Questions to Ask

- How would you describe the timbre of sandpaper?
- We scraped sandpaper with our hands and with our feet. Can you think of any other ways to scrape sandpaper? Open-ended questions like these promote flexible thinking.
- Would anything else make the exact same sound that sandpaper does? Why not?

TIP

Emery boards are also made with aluminum oxide and have a similar timbre to that of sandpaper, only they sound lighter and more delicate. Children may like to experiment with scraping two emery boards against each other.

Discoveries to Make

- Sandpaper has a unique timbre.
- Sandpaper has this timbre because it's made of tiny bits of the mineral aluminum oxide. This relates to structure and function, crosscutting concepts in every domain of science.

THE GUIRO SOUND

The guiro is a staple of Latin American music. Usually made of wood, it has ridges along the side, which are scraped with a mallet to make its characteristic raspy, scratchy sound. The guiro adds a distinctive percussive layer to the rich texture of Latin music.

But you don't need a real guiro to get a similar scritchy-scratchy sound. Other instruments, as well as recycled household instruments, can be excellent substitutes. You can even make your own little guiro out of an index card, as we do in this activity. Science and engineering involve perseverance and cooperation. This activity gives children an opportunity to practice both.

What You'll Need

1 or more guiros

2 rhythm sticks

1 or more plastic bottles with ridges

Large plastic combs

Wire-bound notebooks

Mallets—any kind, one for each instrument

Index cards

Scissors, one pair per child

Large bag

Dry-erase easel or large paper and marker

Activity to Try

1. Have the rhythm sticks in front of you. Everything else should be in a closed bag next to you.

2. Tap and scrape the rhythm sticks a few times. Ask if anyone remembers why there's one smooth stick and one bumpy stick. The bumpy one is needed to make the scrapey sound.

3. Put the sticks back in the bag, and bring out the guiro and a wooden mallet. Tell the children that this instrument is called a guiro. *Guiro* is a Spanish word; these instruments were first played in places such as Puerto Rico and Cuba, where people speak Spanish.

4. Play the guiro for a little while, tapping it with the tip of the mallet and scraping it with the stem.

5. Ask the class how the guiro is like the bumpy rhythm stick. They should realize that there are two similarities—the sound (scratchy, raspy) and the structure (the ridges or bumps). If they notice that the ridges are similar, you can agree that they both have ridges cut into the wood. Their structures are a lot alike. Tell the children that *structure* means how something is built or put together.

6. Pass the guiro, with the mallet, around the circle to allow each child a turn to play it.

7. Show them other things that can be scraped to get a scratchy sound. Bring out the plastic bottle and other items, each with a mallet, and pass them around the circle. You can have a few instruments traveling around the circle at the same time.

8. Encourage the children to try different ways to play the instruments—holding them in the air or on the floor; scraping lightly or forcefully; tapping with the tip of the mallet; or any way they can think of. Remind the children to be careful with the instrument and respectful of the people around them. When they're done, put these instruments to the side.

9. Tell the children that you're going to see whether you can make your own little guiros. Take out an index card and fold it in half. Take out a mallet, and ask what they predict it will sound like if you scrape the folded edge with this mallet. Listen to and acknowledge all responses.

10. Scrape the index card along the folded edge with the mallet. Ask the class what it sounded like. Were their predictions correct?

11. Ask the children how they could make the card sound more like a guiro. Ask what they could do to make it have that scratchy sound. They will probably remember that ridges were cut into the wood of the guiro, and they may suggest that you cut ridges in the folded edge of the card. The children's reasoning may not travel in a straight line, though. They may first want to try cutting small straight lines along the fold. Let them try it. It will make more of a sound, but not a satisfyingly raspy one.

12. Students may suggest unconventional ideas, like scratching the card with their fingernails or putting lots of folded cards together to look like a row of ridges. If their ideas are at all possible, try them out and see what the children think the sounds are like. If they're stuck for ideas, have them study the guiro and the other instruments again and see if they remember how they produced their scratchy sounds.

13. When the children suggest cutting ridges, take out one pair of scissors and try cutting a zigzag line along the edge, about one-half to three-quarters of an inch deep. Then scrape it with a mallet. Ask if that sounded more like a guiro. It does! They figured it out!

14. Children will want to make their own mini-guiros. Give each child a folded card and scissors. They may need you to trace a zigzag line for them to cut along.

15. Pass out the mallets for children to play their new instruments.

Questions to Ask

- How would you describe the sound of the guiro?
- What about the plastic items, such as the bottle? Did they sound the same as the wooden guiro?
- How do you think the structure of the guiro made it have the scratchy sound?
- How did we change the structure of the index card to make it sound different?
- Suppose you were telling someone how to make a guiro-type instrument out of an index card. What would your directions be? Write their directions on the chart, numbering the steps as the students dictate them to you, for instance:
  1. Fold the index card in half.
  2. Cut a zigzag line along the edge.

Discoveries to Make

- The guiro sounds scratchy because of the ridges that are cut into the wood—the structure affects its function.
- Children can change the structures of objects to change their functions.

KEEP THE LEARNING GOING!

If you have a keyboard in the classroom, it's interesting to bring it out soon after the guiro activity and show the children how to do a glissando by sliding the backs of your fingernails of one hand along the keys.

Ask the children how this sound is like the guiro's, and how it's different. You can also do a glissando on a glockenspiel by sliding the tip of a mallet along the bars. Let your students try this—it's really fun.

HOW TO PLAY AN OVEN RACK

You read that right—an oven rack. Recently I experienced the "sound sculptures" of the artist Harry Bertoia. Ever since, I've been looking for a way to adapt some of his unique ideas for young children in an age-appropriate and inexpensive way. Not so easy. Bertoia created his sculptures out of very high-quality metals, such as beryllium copper, making stabile rods that can be played with hands or a soft mallet. My solution, the humble oven rack, is less musical, to say the least. But I think Mr. Bertoia would be pleased to see the delight children take in finding the music in this everyday item.

What You'll Need

Clean oven rack

Cake racks, sink racks, toaster-oven racks, or roaster-pan racks

Various mallets and brushes

Activity to Try

1. Have the mallets and brushes nearby. Hold the oven rack in front of you so that it's standing upright on the floor. Ask if anyone knows what it is. They may know it's an oven rack. Tell the children that you're going to make music with it. Ask them how they think they could do that.

2. The children may suggest strumming the bars with a mallet, a brush, or their fingers; hitting the bars with a mallet; or just banging the rack on the floor. For many young children, this is their go-to method for playing practically any instrument! After listening to their ideas, tell them it's time to see what these ideas sound like.

3. Have two children come up and hold the rack by the top corners, one child on each side. They'll need both hands to keep it steady. The rack should be held about six inches off the floor.

4. Have the first child in the circle play the rack however she wishes.

5. The first time someone strums the bars, whether with a mallet or a brush, you can ask the children what would happen if you held the rack so it's standing right on the floor. Ask if they think it would be louder, softer, or sound the same. When the class has reached a consensus, try it. The sound will be louder and more resonant. After this demonstration, let children who come up to play the rack choose the way they want to play it, in the air or on the ground.

6. Remember to rotate the "rack holders" after every few turns, so each child has a turn to play the rack.

Questions to Ask

- How did the mallet, brush, and finger-strumming sound different? How did they sound the same?
- Can you think of any way that playing the oven rack was like playing a stringed instrument?
- Why do you think the oven rack made different sounds when we held it in the air and when we held it on the floor?

Discovery to Make

When the children stood the rack on the floor, the vibrating bars made the sound vibrate through the floor, creating a deeper, louder, more resonant sound.

> ### KEEP THE LEARNING GOING!
>
> The structure of the oven rack features bars of equal size, spread evenly apart, attached to bars at the bottom. Have your students be on the lookout for objects with similar structures that may be played with lightly strumming fingers or with mallets. These could include a wooden chair with slats, a gate or fence on the playground, or even a plastic baby-proof gate. One of my students recently discovered that strumming the wire binding of a notebook makes a sound "kind of in-between the guiro and the oven rack." If you really want to, you can make music with anything!

R-R-R-RIP!

I let this fantastic learning opportunity go right past me for years. Every time children got distracted by opening and closing Velcro fasteners on their shoes or on bell bracelets, I just felt annoyed by this time-wasting behavior. Luckily, I finally caught on to the fact that children wanted to learn more about these strange—and strange-sounding—fasteners and how they worked.

What You'll Need

10 feet or so of elastic, 1 inch wide

5 feet of Velcro adhesive tape

Scissors

Duct tape

2 large bags

Activity to Try

Ahead of Time:

1. Make a Velcro bracelet for each child in your class. For each bracelet, cut a 9-inch length of elastic. Cut a 2-inch length of the Velcro adhesive tape. Stick the hook side of the Velcro on one end of the elastic, and the loop side on the other end of the elastic, to hold the ends together.

2. Cut 3-inch lengths of the Velcro adhesive tape, one for each bracelet.

3. On half the bracelets, stick the hook side of the Velcro on the outside. On the other half of the bracelets, stick the loop side of the Velcro on the outside.

4. Cut a 6-inch length of Velcro adhesive tape. Pull the two sides apart, and put a piece of duct tape on one end of one half, to make the tape easier for the children to pull apart.

With the Children:

1. Have the bracelets in two closed bags next to you, one for the "hooks" and one for the "loops."

2. Show the class the 6-inch fastened strip, and ask if they know what it is. Some may know, and after you rip it apart, more will recognize it by the sound. Most will call it "that stuff on sneakers" or "scrapers."

3. Say that it's called Velcro. It was invented about seventy years ago by an engineer named George de Mestral, who went for a walk in the woods and noticed little burrs that stuck to his clothes. Burrs are seed cases on some plants that have little prickles all over them. He studied the burrs and saw that the prickles were like little hooks. So he invented these fasteners that work the same way. One side has lots of tiny hooks, and the other side has lots of tiny loops. It's a very strong fastener and it also makes a great sound! Take your time talking about this. Emphasize that the hooks and loops are so tiny that they are hard to see. Once, I rushed through this part and a girl nodded and said, "So it's magic!"

4. Pass the 6-inch strip around the circle for everyone to have a turn ripping it apart and fastening it again.

5. Tell the children that they're going to play a game. It's called Hooks and Loops. Explain that everyone is going to wear one bracelet. Get the bags of bracelets, and take out one bracelet from each bag to show them.

6. Explain that each child will wear a bracelet with tiny hooks on the outside (that's the smooth side) or one with tiny loops (that's the fuzzy side). Divide the class into two groups, and put the hook bracelets on the left wrists of one group and the loop bracelets on the right wrists of the other group. Remind them to keep the bracelets on!

7. Have the children walk slowly around the room, while you sing the following song, to the tune of "The Wheels on the Bus."

The hooks and the loops are walking around,
Walking around, walking around.
The hooks and the loops are walking around,
And now they'll find their partners!

Exploring the Science of Sounds: 100 Musical Activities for Young Children

8. When you stop singing, the children will then look for a child with the opposite side of their Velcro and attach their bracelets, so their wrists are fastened together.

9. When they're all attached, they'll follow the directions as you sing:

> *Now everybody's going to kick their feet,*
>
> *Jump, jump, jump,*
>
> *Clap, clap, clap!* (Clap with nonattached hands)
>
> *Now everybody's going to kick their feet,*
>
> *And jump, and clap, and r-r-rip!* (Everyone rip apart from their partner)

10. You can help cue this by ripping the six-inch strip apart.

11. Play again, with everyone finding a new partner.

12. After the game, collect the bracelets.

Questions to Ask

- What do you think the Velcro is made of? It's made of plastic.

- How long do you think the engineer worked on the hook-and-loop idea until he had the finished invention? I like to ask this because children don't often realize how much hard work goes into creating something. It took de Mestral more than eight years to come up with his finished product!

- Do you think scientists get other ideas for inventions by observing plants and animals?

- What if we tried to stick a "hook" side to another "hook" side? Would it stick?" Most often, children aren't sure about this, so try it out. Also try sticking the "loop" sides together.

Discoveries to Make

- Velcro fasteners have a unique sound because of the way they're made and the material they're made of. This is an example of the crosscutting concepts of structure and function.

- Scientists can get good ideas for inventions by observing plants and animals.

Learning about inventions inspired by plants and animals can help children observe the world around them in a whole new way. Find out about some cool nature-inspired inventions here: https://www.theguardian.com/sustainable-business/sustainable-fashion-blog/nature-fabrics-fashion-industry-biomimicry

THE TAP GLOVES GUESSING GAME

I just discovered tap gloves! No, not those gloves that let you tap your smartphone screen. I mean gloves to tap dance with! I sewed an assortment of colorful old buttons to the fingertips of dollar-store children's gloves, and guess what? They're really fun! Tapping my fingers on a tabletop got much more interesting. And tapping on countertops. And pots and pans. And all over my house, until party-pooping family members took them away.

For this activity, I use the tap gloves as a way to engage students in an unusual exploration of different timbres. They not only finger-tap on a variety of surfaces, but they also practice listening to and distinguishing the surfaces' timbres.

What You'll Need

1 pair of children's knit gloves

10 buttons, half-inch across or a bit larger

Needle and thread (adult use only)

Aluminum foil

Waxed paper

Large, long wooden block

Large, plastic container lid

Large bag

Activity to Try

Ahead of Time:

Sew the buttons to the fingertips of the gloves. Young children tend to tap their fingers with their hands held flat rather than curved, so you'll want to sew the buttons to the bottoms of the fingertips. This way, children will get the maximum sound from their tapping.

With the Children:

1. Have the foil and the other materials in a closed bag next to you.
2. Put on the gloves and wave your hands around so the class can see the buttons. Ask if anyone can guess why the gloves have buttons on them. Listen to and acknowledge the children's guesses. You'll probably get a lot of guesses, and that's good. It means they're engaged and curious. The more guesses the better!

Exploring the Science of Sounds: 100 Musical Activities for Young Children

3. Tell the children that, as some of them may have guessed, the gloves are musical instruments. Sometimes children will ask me where I got them or how I made them. Explain how you made the gloves.

4. Take off the gloves and bring out the materials from the bag. Set them out, side by side, on the floor in front of you.

5. Explain the activity. The children are going to try to fool you. You're going to turn around and close your eyes, and one of them will put on the gloves and tap on the foil, the waxed paper, the wooden block, or the plastic lid (tap on each to demonstrate). Then you'll try to guess which material they tapped on, based on the timbre you hear.

6. Going around the circle, give several children turns to try to fool you. (I usually "get stumped" or at least take a while to decide on one or two, to make it more fun.)

7. After a few turns, have a child take over your role, trying to guess the tapped material, while the next child in the circle does the tapping.

8. Continue in this way until everyone has had a turn to either tap or guess.

Questions to Ask

- Which material had the loudest timbre? Which had the softest?
- Which material was the easiest to tell apart from the others?
- How were you able to tell which material was being tapped?

Discovery to Make

Children can distinguish the timbres of different materials using only their hearing.

KEEP THE LEARNING GOING!

After the activity, keep the tap gloves in the music center. Children can use them to freely explore different timbres around the room or to play the guessing game with friends.

DRAWING TIMBRES

Hearing and distinguishing voices, instruments, and noises of similar timbres and of different timbres is an important part of how we experience sound. It's the difference between hearing a piano duet and a symphony for an orchestra. In this activity, children will draw with different colors to represent the timbres they hear.

What You'll Need

5 different musical instruments

1 shaker

1 triangle

Blanket

Plain white paper

Crayons

Activity to Try

Ahead of Time:

1. The children will be sitting at tables for this activity, with you seated at the head of one table. Hang the blanket over chairs behind where you will sit, to create a curtain.

2. Line up the instruments on the floor in a row behind the curtain where children can't see them. Keep the shaker and the triangle next to you.

With the Children:

1. Review the different objects and timbres children have been listening to. Ask the children which objects had bright, sharp timbres and which had dry, dull timbres. Ask if they remember which objects were hit, which were plucked, and which were shaken.

2. Tell the children you'd like them to listen carefully to what you're about to do. Play the shaker briefly and then the triangle. Ask them if they could hear the difference in timbre.

3. Tell them there are instruments behind the curtain. Some children will play them one at a time (they'll take turns), and the rest will try to tell when the timbre changes.

4. Have a child go behind the curtain and sit behind one of the instruments. Have four more children follow, one at a time, so there's no squabbling over the instruments.

5. Pass out paper to the remaining children and have crayons available on the tables.

6. Explain the directions: When they hear a sound, they should start drawing with one color. They can draw a line, a shape, or anything they want. But when they hear a different timbre, they should stop and draw with a different color. Every time they hear a new timbre, they should draw with another color.

7. Have the children behind the curtain play their instruments one at a time. Each child can keep playing for a little while, to give the other children time to draw.

8. If there's time, repeat until each child has had a turn to play behind the curtain.

Questions to Ask

- Did every timbre sound different? How?

- Could you tell what any of the instruments were? What instruments did you hear?

- Would any of you like to tell us about your drawing and how you drew the different timbres you heard?

- Were you able to show all the different timbres you heard with different colors?

- We used a different color for each timbre. Can you think of another way we could show that we heard different timbres? Some of my students have suggested drawing the instrument they hear playing, making a movement with their hands or bodies, or pretending to play the instrument they hear.

Discoveries to Make

- Children can hear different timbres, even when they can't see the instruments.

- Children can represent the different timbres they hear by drawing with different colors.

> ### KEEP THE LEARNING GOING!
>
> If children suggested new ways to show the instrumental timbres they hear, try out these ideas, if possible. Lead a similar activity to this one but with children pretending to play the instruments they hear or raising their hands briefly every time they hear a new timbre or using other ways to communicate their understanding of changing timbres.

ROBOT DANCE

I came up with this game years ago, and it's one of my students' favorites. Even when I repeat it often, I don't get tired of it. It's always fun to watch the children laugh while they invent strange-looking robot dance moves. But recently it occurred to me that the metal timbre is really an integral part of the game. (Whoever heard of a robot made of wood?) The Robot Dance is a perfect example of the dramatic and expressive qualities of the timbre of metal.

What You'll Need

Egg carton

1 roll of heavy-duty aluminum foil, the extra-wide size

Newspaper

Construction paper

Tape

Large bag

Recording of music robots would dance to, such as "Alien Robot Party" by Fred Clark or "Outta Space" by Billy Preston

Activity to Try

Ahead of Time:

Cover the egg carton with the aluminum foil. This will be your robot remote control.

With the Children:

1. Have the foil, newspaper, and construction paper next to you. Have the robot remote control in a closed bag.
2. Tell the class that they're going to be dancing like robots. And to feel more like robots, they're going to make special robot hats!
3. Set out the foil, newspaper, and construction paper in front of you. Ask the students to think for a minute about which material they should use to make robot hats, and why. They will usually agree that the foil is most suitable, but sometimes there are outliers. Let them use the material they prefer.

4. Tear off a sheet of foil, about 1 1/2 feet long. Put it on your head and crumple up the sides until it will stay on your head. Enjoy the silliness of it. You could say something like, "Now-I-am-a-ro-bot," in a monotone voice and move your arms stiffly.

5. Remind them that they are free to make the hat look any way they want—it doesn't have to look just like yours. Those choosing newspaper or construction paper may need tape to construct a hat.

6. When the hats are ready, have everyone stand up and ask them to show you their robot dance moves. Encourage them to use their heads, hands, and legs, not just their arms. Admire their moves enthusiastically.

7. Explain the game: When the music starts, the children are going to start dancing. But there's a catch. Show them your robot remote control. If you (gently) bop them on the head with the remote control, they have to freeze! Also, tell them they should pay attention to what it sounds like when the remote control bops their robot hat.

8. Start the music (not too loud), and dance with them for a bit. Then, start bopping children to freeze them. Continue until everyone has been bopped.

Questions to Ask

- How would you describe the sound of the remote control bopping your robot hat?

- What do you think might be inside the robot remote control? (Actually, in my experience, children always ask me about this before I get a chance to ask them. I'm including this question, even though it doesn't relate to the subject of timbre, because it's one that engages students in analytical thinking and provokes discussion. Often, someone asks if it's a real remote control, and others say no, of course it isn't. So they get into a back-and-forth about relevant details, such as the object's lightness, its lack of buttons or "places for batteries," and so on. This happens a lot and it's a fruitful, thought-provoking, and usually loud conversation.

- What could we change if we wanted a different sound when we bop the hat?

- Imagine you were wearing woolly winter hats and I bopped you with a mitten. Would you still feel like a pretend robot?

Discovery to Make

Using different timbres can add fun and humor to an activity, in this case the timbre of foil.

KEEP THE LEARNING GOING!

This is such a fun and exciting game that children often want to play it again right away. You can vary it by playing it in reverse, bopping the frozen robots to unfreeze them and let them start dancing again. And of course, you can have children take turns being the "bopper."

THE MYSTERY MUSIC CAN

This has been one of my students' favorite activities for years. I always use the same green, plastic coffee can for the game, so when they see me bring it out they know what's coming and get excited. Children love guessing games, but of course this is a special kind of guessing game—one in which they're making "educated guesses." These guesses should be grounded in their knowledge and sensory experiences.

What You'll Need

Plastic coffee can

Variety of items, such as small jingle bells, wooden and/or plastic beads, paper clips, sand, wooden blocks, twist ties, plastic tags from bread loaves, cotton puffs, small plastic manipulatives, plastic bottle caps, small bouncy balls, plastic building bricks, erasers, small pebbles, acorns (unless someone has an allergy to tree nuts), seashells, and so on

Activity to Try

Ahead of Time:

Fill the container halfway with one of the items you have gathered.

With the Children:

1. Start things off with a flourish, bringing out the can and announcing, "And now it's time for the Mystery Music Can!" Wonder aloud what could be in the can. Give the can a shake and look surprised and intrigued. Ask the children if they think it will sound the same if you shake it again. Listen to their responses. Try it so children can hear that it does sound the same.

2. Pass the can around the circle. Each child can shake it for a few moments and listen to the sound carefully. Remind them not to open it and not to shake it too hard—they could accidentally hit themselves in the face or bump the can on the floor, making the lid pop off. Children should shake it just hard enough to hear the sound. They may want to shake it near their ears.

3. After everyone's had a turn, ask the children if they think they know what might be inside. Children should raise their hand before calling out. They'll need to be reminded of this because they get very excited and can't wait to tell everybody their guesses.

4. When everyone who has a guess has shared it with the group, reveal the contents of the can. So that the whole group can see more easily, I usually pour some of the items out in my hand rather than just holding out the lidless can.

Questions to Ask

- You've asked them what they thought was in the can. But remember to ask, too, how they came to their conclusion. Listen to their ideas.

- Then you might say something like, "Even though he didn't get the right answer, Vihan made a very good guess, because it showed he could tell the things inside were small and hard." This kind of comment communicates to children that thinking logically is valuable and important.

- What were you thinking of when you tried to figure out what was inside?

- Did you think of other things you'd heard that sounded like it?

Discovery to Make

Children can identify sounds by careful listening and by thinking of other objects they've heard that have the same or a similar sound.

KEEP THE LEARNING GOING!

If this game becomes a favorite, as it has with many of my classes, children may enjoy making Mystery Music Cans for you to listen to. They can take turns bringing items to school in their backpacks and, while you're not looking, putting the items in the can. Then at circle time, the class can see if you can guess what's inside. Model your critical-thinking skills: "Hmm. It's very loud, so I know it isn't something soft like a sock. It sounds like many hard little things, but the can feels light, so I don't think it's rocks," and so on.

CHAPTER FOUR

LOUD AND SOFT SOUNDS: THE SCIENCE OF LOUDNESS

Ask the group for ideas on why some sounds are loud and some are soft. They may think loud sounds are bigger, harder, or stronger, or that they're made by big things. They may think soft sounds are smaller or come from small things. Accept all responses with a nod, a "thank you," "could be," or another noncommittal acknowledgement. At this point, there are no right or wrong answers. Allow each child who wants to contribute an idea a chance to respond. Tell the children that they had interesting ideas, and that you're all going to be doing some exploring and experimenting to find out exactly what makes some sounds loud and some sounds soft.

KEY CONCEPTS

- The more forcefully a sound is made, the louder it will sound.

- The nearer a sound is to you, the louder it will sound.

The proportional relationship between force and loudness, explored in some of these activities, is simplified but scientifically correct. A fuller explanation of the relationship is that increased force causes increased amplitude, measured by the maximum displacement of particles in the sound wave, which in turn causes increased loudness. For more information see The Physics Classroom site, http://www.physicsclassroom.com/Class/waves.

THE MARCHING MINUTE CHALLENGE

Following the principle of "starting where the children are," start with doing something loud—because children love the chance to show you how loud they can be. Probably the loudest sound children can make (aside from yelling, which I decided against for obvious reasons) is marching their feet. This activity is designed to get children thinking about how they make their marching feet sound loud—or soft.

What You'll Need

Recorded march music, such as "March" from *The Nutcracker Suite* by Pyotr Tchaikovsky or "Radetzky March" by Johann Strauss, Sr.

Watch or a stopwatch app

Activity to Try

1. Have the children stand in a circle. Tell them that this activity is about exploring loud sounds and soft sounds. Explain that in a minute, you're going to ask them to march in place as loudly as they can for half a minute, and that you want them to pay attention to how it feels to march loudly.

2. Start the music and the timer, and ask the children to start marching loudly with you and to pay attention to how it feels to march loudly. You might want to count out "1,2,3,4, 1,2,3,4" and so on, at first, to help them keep a beat as they march. Some children will definitely try to impress you with their loudness, and that's good—they'll feel the force of their movements. Stop after thirty seconds.

3. Ask the class to march as softly as they can for half a minute and to pay attention to how it feels.

4. Have the children sit back down.

Questions to Ask

- What did it feel like to march loudly?
- How did your legs and feet feel?
- Did it feel any different to march softly? How?
- If you were explaining to someone how they should move their legs to make a loud-sounding march, what would you tell them?
- How would you tell them to move to make a soft-sounding march?
- What kind of movement would you say creates loud sounds?
- What kind of movement creates soft sounds?

Exploring the Science of Sounds: 100 Musical Activities for Young Children

Discovery to Make

Strong, forceful movement creates loud sounds, and weak, less forceful movement creates soft sounds. Restate this for the class in the vocabulary they used—for instance, they might have said *hard* instead of *strong* and *small* or *soft* instead of *weak*. Doing this reinforces that this principle is something they discovered for themselves. Then you can add the scientific term. For instance, you could say, "Yes, our legs marched harder. They used more force. More force makes louder sounds."

TIP

Listen to every child who wants to answer a question. Even if the "right" answer has already been stated, allow other children to answer the question in their own way. They may say— as one boy did—that marching loud feels "like a monster." That's okay. Accepting their descriptions affirms for them that their individual thinking processes are valued.

 MAKING OTHER LOUD AND SOFT SOUNDS WITH OUR FEET

In "The Marching Minute Challenge," children discovered that using more force, or strength, when marching will produce louder sounds than using less force. Here, they're going to build on that discovery and use previous knowledge of different ways they can make sounds with their feet to explore more ways to create loud and soft sounds. They'll also see if all the sounds they can make with their feet can be made both loudly and softly.

What You'll Need

No materials needed

Activity to Try

1. With the children standing in a circle, review the discovery they made that more force, or strength, creates louder sounds. Starting a review with questions, such as "Does anyone remember when we made marching sounds? How did we do that? How did we make loud sounds? How did we make soft sounds?" encourages the children to think. Intervene only if they need some hints.

2. Ask the class to think about different ways they can move their feet loudly and softly. They might suggest stomping, jumping, kicking, tiptoeing, galloping, and walking. Encourage them to think of ways to use each part of the foot—the toes, the heels, the sides, the balls of the feet. Suggest moving in new ways. Can they move their feet to the front and back? Side to side? Can they stomp while sitting down? Accept each response and have the group try to perform each movement both loudly and softly.

3. Have the children sit back down.

Questions to Ask

- What was the loudest sound we made? What was the quietest?

- Do you still feel that you need more strength or force to make loud sounds, and less force to make softer sounds?

- When we jumped, making sounds with both feet at the same time, was it louder or softer than when we made sounds with one foot at a time, as in stomping or galloping? If they're not sure, or if children disagree, let them try these movements again.

- Were we able to make each of the movements both loudly and softly, or were there some that only made one kind of sound? If they're not sure, mention the movements one by one, having the group try them again if necessary.

- Why do you think we were able to make the loudest sound by jumping? If they need more help, you might ask, "When we jump, are we using just our feet?"

Discoveries to Make

- Tiptoeing can't make a loud sound. Since it uses only a small part of the foot, it can't be as strong as a movement using the whole foot. It doesn't use as much force.

- Jumping can make a louder sound than other sounds we make with our feet, not only because you're using both feet, but also because the whole body is hitting the floor, which uses more force.

- Kicking doesn't make a sound, since the kicking foot is going into the air instead of hitting the floor.

CLAPPING LOUDLY AND SOFTLY

Oddly enough, I've found that this activity is a little challenging for some children. Clapping their hands to music is such a familiar, everyday action that they don't really think about how loudly they're clapping. So clapping softly isn't as easy as it sounds. That's why I have the students think about animals—they can use their imaginations to help them control their movements.

What You'll Need

Recording of music with a steady beat (see "Suggested Recordings of Instrumental Music" on page 190)

Activity to Try

1. Ask the children how they used their feet to make loud and soft sounds in the "Making Other Loud and Soft Sounds with Our Feet" activity. They should remember that using more force created louder sounds than using less force.

2. Tell them that they're going to be clapping to music, pretending to be different animals. Can they think of an animal that would clap very loudly? How about an animal that would clap softly? Listen to each response and use their suggestions as you lead the activity.

3. Start the music, playing it rather softly so the class can hear the beat even when they're clapping very quietly. Call out directions for how to clap, such as "Let's clap like elephants!" "Now, let's try clapping like a chipmunk," and so on.

4. The activity needs to move along so it doesn't get monotonous, but you don't want to switch animals so fast that children get confused or frustrated trying to keep up. Observe how well they're able to follow along. You can always switch animals at a slower or faster pace if you need to.

Questions to Ask

- Did clapping work the same way as using our feet? Did we use more force to make louder sounds?

- How did you use more force when you clapped? Children may say they just clapped harder, or they may say they moved their arms more. If they're not sure, have someone come up to the front and clap both softly and loudly, asking the class to watch the child's movements carefully. Ask, "Did her hands and arms move more when she clapped loudly?"

- Can we clap very loudly using just our hands? Model this by holding your wrists together and clapping, and ask the children to try it.

- Can we be louder when we can use our arms? Try this with the group, too.

- What did we need to do to clap very loudly?

- Does using our arms when we clap give us more strength and more force?

Discoveries to Make

- To clap loudly, we need the extra force of our arms not just our hands.
- Using more force creates louder sounds, and using less force creates softer sounds. This relates to the crosscutting concepts of scale, proportion, and quantity, which relate to all domains of science.

> ### KEEP THE LEARNING GOING!
>
> This activity can be continued throughout the day, especially during transitions. You could suggest that children clap like butterflies, or ask them to show you how a whale would clap. You can also ask them for ideas for other animals that they could clap like. Once in a while, reinforce the main concept by saying something like, "Wow! We had to use a lot of force to clap like whales!"

CONDUCTING LOUD AND SOFT BELLS

In this game, children will combine their knowledge of playing bells loudly and softly with a fun challenge—responding to the visual cues of a conductor. The child who conducts gets an opportunity to lead the group, to decide when the group will play loudly or softly, and to communicate directions using only hand signals, which is also a fun challenge! You may want to play this game a few days in a row, so that every child in the class has a chance to conduct.

What You'll Need

Bell bracelets—one per child

Activity to Try

1. Ask the children if they've ever seen a conductor leading a band or orchestra. If some have, ask about how the conductor tells the band how to play. If not, explain that a conductor uses only her hands, and sometimes a stick called a *baton*, to lead.

2. Tell the class that they're going to play in a band of bells, and you're going to be the conductor. Demonstrate the signals for "play more loudly" (raising hands slowly in the air, palms up) and "play more softly" (lowering hands slowly, palms down). Have the children try this with you.
Pass out the bells and conduct the group with the hand signals, giving plenty of time between changing signals. Continue for about a minute.

3. Ask if any of the children would like to take a turn being the conductor. If time permits, give several children turns.

4. Collect the bells.

Questions to Ask

- How did it feel to follow hand signals, instead of someone telling you directions in words?
- Was it easy or difficult to follow the hand signals? Why?
- Did you use your hearing to follow directions or one of your other senses?

Discoveries to Make

- A conductor can tell a band to play loudly or softly by using hand signals.
- Children can follow a leader's directions or lead a group themselves using only visual signals.

> **KEEP THE LEARNING GOING!**
>
> Ask the group if they can think of other ways a conductor might signal "loud" and "soft." Then try out the various ideas they come up with.

 SSHHHH!

"Suddenly . . ." Isn't that the best part of any story? Young children love anything sudden—"freezing" in a freeze dance, puppets popping out from behind your back, sudden loud sounds and sudden soft sounds. They get so excited waiting for the sudden quietness in this game that they're super-focused on your verbal cue of "Sshh!" Children also enjoy using more and more force to make the bells get louder and louder.

What You'll Need

Bell bracelets, the kind with Velcro—one per child

Activity to Try

1. Tell the class they're going to play a very fun game about loud and soft, using bells. But they're going to wear the bells a little differently today. Instead of just holding them or putting them around their wrists, they're going to use them to attach themselves to each other!

2. Starting with the student on your right, put a bell bracelet around her right wrist. Then put one around the next student's left wrist and through the first student's bracelet, like links in a chain. Continue around the circle until everyone's connected—you too!

3. Show the children how to play the singing game. It starts with everyone moving their hands just a little bit, like a soft knocking motion. Sing the following to the tune of "Hurry, Hurry, Drive the Fire Truck":

> *Bells are jingling very softly,*
>
> *Bells are jingling very softly,*
>
> *Bells are jingling very softly,*
>
> *Very softly, Sshh!* (On "Sshh!" the children should hold their hands still, so bells can't be heard.)

4. Next verses:

> *Bells are jingling just a little louder . . .* (move hands more, but still gently, from wrists)
>
> *Bells are jingling even louder . . .* (move arms from elbows down)
>
> *Bells are jingling very loud now . . .* (move arms from the shoulder)

5. Collect the bells after the game.

Questions to Ask

- How did we make a soft sound? Did we use a lot of force or a little?
- How did we make louder sounds?
- Did the bells sound louder and louder as we moved our arms more forcefully?

Discovery to Make

Playing bells with more and more force makes them sound louder and louder.

KEEP THE LEARNING GOING!

Challenge the group to come up with a way to make an even louder sound with the bells in this game. If a suggestion is doable—for instance, jumping while shaking bells so the force of the whole body is used—give it a try.

Exploring the Science of Sounds: 100 Musical Activities for Young Children

WILL ALUMINUM FOIL SOUND LOUDER WHEN SHAKEN WITH TWO FINGERS OR WITH BOTH HANDS?

The learning in this experiment seems redundant; children seem to have already learned that more force equals louder sound. But concepts aren't learned in a day. Multiple experiences with a concept are important to reinforce and strengthen children's learning. And you know what's really, really, fun? Playing with aluminum foil! The sound made by shaking a sheet of aluminum foil is exciting, dramatic, and irresistible to young children.

What You'll Need

12"-wide aluminum foil, torn into 12" sheets, one per child

Activity to Try

1. Explain that you're all going to do an experiment. You're going to try to find out if you'll make a louder sound when you shake aluminum foil while pinching it between your thumb and pointer finger or while you're holding it with both hands. Demonstrate both positions with your hands, without holding the foil.

2. Ask the children which way they think will be louder and why. After hearing a few answers, take a vote: Which way does the class think will be louder? Tell them that this is their prediction, or hypothesis.

3. Place a sheet of foil in front of each child. Ask them not to touch the foil yet.

4. When everyone has foil, ask the children to pick up their sheets with a pinch of their thumb and pointer finger. For a little added drama, you could say, "On the count of three, we'll all shake it. One, two, three—Shake!" Let them shake the foil for a while. Encourage them to shake it as loudly as they can.

5. Repeat, having the children use both hands to hold the foil.

6. Take another vote—which way do most children think was louder?

7. To extend this activity, tear off a four-foot-long sheet of foil, and have children take turns shaking it, with one child on each end. This is really loud and children love it.

Questions to Ask

- Why do you think the both-hands way was louder than the two-finger way?
- Do you think you could shake the foil softly while holding it with both hands? Have them try this out.
- How did you shake it differently to make the softer sound?
- What happens to a sound when we use more force to make it? Does it get softer or louder?

Discovery to Make

It isn't only marching feet that sound louder when using more force. Using more force will make another sound—and maybe all sounds—louder.

> ### ALGEBRA IN PRESCHOOL?
>
> When children make a generalization of this type, that using more force makes sounds louder, they're thinking mathematically. They're thinking in terms of a proportional relationship: if force increases, loudness will increase. There's actually more to loudness than the force used to create a sound, as you'll see in future activities, but this kind of reasoning is important for the development of children's critical-thinking skills, early math and science skills, and their eventual understanding of algebraic concepts.

 MAKING LOUD AND SOFT SOUNDS WITH WATER

Water is a wonderful, developmentally appropriate medium for young children to explore. Water is everywhere in their lives—they drink it, they feel it fall down as rain, they use it to bathe and brush their teeth. There's hardly any substance children are more familiar with. So they have a great base of knowledge about water to build on. But they probably haven't thought a lot about all the different sounds they can make using water. In this activity, students will learn about water from a whole new perspective. This is a new experience for most young children, and it's wonderful to watch them bring "fresh ears" to something adults take for granted. They always come up with new and original ideas for water sounds.

What You'll Need

Water table

Plastic spoons and cups

Plastic basters, squirt bottles, eye droppers

Spray bottle

Funnel

Colander

Toothbrush

Waterproof smocks

Water

Activity to Try

1. Tell the children that they'll be exploring all the loud and soft sounds they can make with water.

2. Two or three children at a time can work at the water table. They can do research on how they can make loud and soft sounds using the cups and other objects to pour into the water or the other objects. Tell them they'll want to remember what they did so they can talk about it in the group later. Encourage children to invent new ways to pour, squirt, dribble, and strain water with the various objects. They can also tap or splash water gently with upside-down cups, the bottoms of spoons, or other items.

3. After the investigating, bring the whole group back to the circle for a discussion. Try not to wait too long between the water-table research and the discussion—you want children to have their experience fresh in their minds.

Questions to Ask

- Were you able to make both loud and soft sounds with the water? Can you describe some of the loud and soft sounds you made?

- Did you know beforehand that certain things you tried would be loud? How did you know?

- Did anyone use the spray bottle? How would you describe the sounds it could make?

- Which kinds of objects made the loudest sounds? Why?

- Which kinds of objects made the softest sounds? Why?

- Was there a difference between how you made loud sounds and how you made soft sounds?

- Does water sound different from solid objects, such as bells and rhythm sticks? Does it have a different timbre? Why? If they've forgotten, ask them how sound moves differently through air, water, and solids.

Discoveries to Make

- Large objects tend to make the loudest sounds, because they can hold more water and use the most force when the water inside them hits the water in the table.

- Smaller objects tend to make softer sounds, because they hold less water.

- Just like solid objects, water makes louder sounds with more forceful movement. Pouring water forcefully makes a loud sound, while squirting or dribbling it makes softer sounds.

- Water sounds different from solid objects; it has a different timbre.

> If children disagree or even argue about their findings, that's fine. Remember that science is a creative and ongoing process. Children need to understand science not as a collection of facts but as a dynamic, ongoing discussion of ideas.

 WATER MUSIC

Music created expressly for relaxation and peaceful sleep often features the sounds of gentle rain, rhythmic splashing waves, and waterfalls. Water is a wonderful "instrument" to accompany calm, soothing music—it's a natural relaxant. In the "Making Loud and Soft Sounds with Water" activity, children explored water with the sole purpose of discovering the loud and soft sounds they could create with it. Now they'll have the opportunity to use their discoveries in an expressive, musical way.

What You'll Need

3-4 large soup pots

Plastic sheet or tablecloth

Plastic spoons and cups

Plastic basters, squirt bottles, eye dropper

Spray bottle

Funnel

Colander

Toothbrush

Waterproof smocks

Water

Dry-erase easel or large paper and marker

Recording of peaceful instrumental music, such as "Tribal Jungle Music—Fountain of Youth" by Derek and Brandon Fiechter, "Clair de Lune" by Claude Debussy, and "Sunset Ceremony" by David and Steve Gordon

Activity to Try

1. Tell the class that they'll be exploring water again today but in a new way. First, they're going to listen to a piece of music.

2. Remind the children to stay quiet and listen very carefully to the way the music sounds. For children who find it very difficult to sit still, I sometimes suggest that they rest their hands on their legs and gently tap their index fingers to the beat of the music. I've found that just having something to do with their hands can help them focus.

3. Play the music for about two minutes. Have the children describe what they heard. Their answers may be short and vague, for example, "It sounded like nighttime." Gently help them expand their responses. You could ask, "How was it like nighttime? Was it quiet? Did it remind you of things you see at night?" You may hear unexpected answers, such as "It was spooky" or "Scary." Young children who are used to hearing cheerful, fast, bouncy music may react like this at first to slow-paced or classical music, and that's okay.

4. Ask the class to think back to the sounds they created in the "Ways to Make Loud and Soft Sounds with Water" activity, using the cups and other items. Ask them which water sounds could be used to accompany this music that would fit the mood of the music.

5. Write or draw four of their ideas on a chart. It may look like this:

> Spray
>
> Pour water like a waterfall
>
> Tap water gently with upside down cup
>
> Stir water gently

6. Bring out the plastic sheet and the cups and other water table items. Tell the class that they're going to create a new piece of music by using their water sounds to accompany the music. Fill the pots halfway and set them out in a row on the sheet.

7. Explain that they'll play the sounds one at a time at first and then all together at the end. Tell them you'll nod to them when it's their turn to play. Choose two children to play each sound at one of the pots.

8. Remind the other children to be good listeners. Start the music. Quietly point to the chart, and nod to the players whose sound will start. Let them play for a little while and move on to the next sound. When all the sounds are done, have them all play together.

9. Stop the music and thank the musicians for their playing and for cooperating with each other so well. Thank the audience for listening respectfully.

10. Repeat to give each child a turn to be a "water musician."

TIP

To bring out even more creative thinking, ask the children to think of a title for the piece of music they composed. When they agree on a title, write it at the top of the chart.

Questions to Ask

- What did the music sound like with the water sounds?

- Do you think the sounds went well with the feeling of the music?

- People who create pieces of music by deciding how the instruments will play and what sounds they will make are called composers. Today, you were composers. How did you decide which sounds to use?

Discoveries to Make

- Water sounds can be used expressively to make music.

- Children can compose music by deciding which sounds will be played.

EVEN ONE RAINDROP

Early in my experiences with young children, I learned two of their favorite kinds of songs. One was the kind that gets faster and faster as it goes along. The other was the kind that gets louder and louder. I wouldn't want to lead this kind of activity every day but once in a while it helps children blow off steam in a harmless way. And in this activity, they're also relearning the relationship between force and loudness in a new context.

What You'll Need

Aluminum foil

Activity to Try

1. Bring out the aluminum foil and say that the children will use it to pretend to be raindrops. Tear off a sheet of foil eight to ten inches wide and place it in front of you. Wonder out loud how you could make the sound of rain–not a lot of rain but just one raindrop at a time. Ask if anyone has an idea.

2. There may be a few ideas; try out any reasonable suggestions. Chances are, though, that after a while, they'll settle on the plan of having one finger, usually a pointer finger, tap the foil very slowly. (If the class prefers another way, that's fine. I try not to tell children how to pretend to be something.)

3. Give each child a small sheet of foil, and have everyone try out the slow tapping. Remind them not to try to flatten out their piece of foil–that changes the sound.

4. Tell them you're going to sing a song about raindrops that gets louder as it goes along, but it starts out very soft. Prepare them for the ending by reminding them that there's a difference between singing loudly and shouting. Even though you'll be singing really loudly at the end, you're not going to be shouting. Some groups may need to practice singing loudly rather than shouting.

5. Have one child be a "raindrop," tapping slowly on her foil, while you sing (to the tune of "If You're Happy and You Know It"):

> *Oh, even one raindrop makes a sound.* (drop drop)
>
> *Oh, even one raindrop makes a sound.* (drop drop)
>
> *Oh, even if it's quiet* (put finger on lips like the "ssh" gesture)
>
> *When it falls to the ground,*
>
> *Oh, even one raindrop makes a sound.* (drop drop)

6. If you have a very small group, say ten children or fewer, you can add one child at a time to the "raindrops," singing, ". . . even two raindrops . . . ," "even three raindrops . . . ," and so on. With a larger group, you can add two or even three children at a time.

7. As you add "raindrops," you can sing louder, too. When everyone is "raining" at the end of the song, you can sing "Oh, lots and lots of raindrops make a sound!" for your last verse, singing nice and loudly!

8. Collect the aluminum foil after the song.

TIP

For this activity to be most effective, make sure everyone is "raining" at about the same loudness. If one child is trying to rain really hard—sometimes they get carried away—gently remind her that each of us is just one little raindrop.

Questions to Ask

- When only (name of the first child) was being a raindrop, was the sound loud or soft?
- How did the "raining" sound at the end?
- Why did our "rain" sound louder at the end of the song?
- Did all the little sounds of each person's playing add up to a big sound?

Discoveries to Make

- Many small sounds add up to a lot of sound.
- Louder sounds are created by using more force—in this case, the force of more and more small forces added together.

 CRASH

For young children (some more than others), there's something innately satisfying about knocking things down. How often have you seen children spend several minutes building a tower of blocks only to gleefully knock it over seconds later? They feel strong and powerful when they can create and destroy. I think that's why they like this game so much. Well, that, and it also makes a lot of noise.

What You'll Need

15 coffee cans with lids

Playground ball—the rubber kind is best for this game

Large bag or box

Activity to Try

1. Play this game outdoors on a hard surface. Have all the coffee cans in a bag or box nearby. With the class gathered around you, place one of the cans, standing upright, on the ground about 6 to 8 feet away.

2. Tell the children you're going to do something to the can, and you want them to listen. Roll the ball to knock the can down.

3. Ask the children to describe the sound they heard when the can fell down. They may say "a crash," or just, "It sounded like something falling down."

4. Bring out two more cans. Set them on the ground side by side, and set the first can on top. Wonder aloud what kind of noise you'd make if you knocked down all three cans. If children don't shout, "A louder noise!" right away, ask them directly if they think the noise would be louder or softer than the first crash.

5. Ask a child to roll the ball to knock down the cans; she can go as close as she'd like. After she knocks them down, ask the children if their prediction was correct.

6. Ask the children if they think knocking down an even bigger stack of cans would make an even louder sound. Build the next stack using three cans for the bottom row, two cans on top of those, and one can on the very top. Have the children count all the cans in the stack. Choose a child to knock it down.

7. Continue the game until the children have knocked down the fifteen-can stack.

8. Of course, after the activity, you can keep the bag of cans for children to play the game when they wish, with supervision.

Questions to Ask

- When I knocked one can down, did it make a sound?
- We knocked down stacks of three, six, ten, and fifteen cans. Which made the loudest crash?
- Did each can hitting the ground make a sound?
- As we added more cans, did the force of all the cans add up to more force and louder sounds?

Discoveries to Make

- Knocking down more and more cans makes louder and louder crashes.
- The forces of all the individual cans hitting the ground add up to a larger force and a louder sound.

KEEP THE LEARNING GOING!

If children show interest in making even louder sounds, bring twenty-one coffee cans outside the next day. Set up a bottom row of six cans, and let children build the stack. Encourage them to figure out how to do it. Then it's time to knock it down!

USING BELLS TO ACCOMPANY "THE CRICKETS"

This charming, funny little story, found in the book *Mouse Soup* by Arnold Lobel, is a natural for music time. Most of the characters are crickets, who are naturally musical insects. The plot revolves around sound—too much sound, in this case. Children love the silliness as exuberant crickets misunderstand a mouse who's trying to sleep. The increase in noise (or music, depending on your point of view) produced by more and more crickets perfectly illustrates the relationship between force and loudness.

What You'll Need

Mouse Soup by Arnold Lobel

Bell bracelets, one per child (except the "mouse")

Activity to Try

1. Before using the bells in a performance of "The Crickets," read the story to the class. Be sure every child understands the humor. Ask them why the crickets kept making more music, even when the mouse asked them not to.

2. It's a very short story, so you can do the musical performance right afterward. Explain that you're going to act out the story, using bells to make a sound like crickets chirping. Ask for a volunteer to play the mouse (you can always play this again so more people can get turns to play the lead). You'll also need a "first cricket" and "second cricket."

3. Pass out bell bracelets to all the crickets. Remind them that until the end, they don't chirp very loudly. Practice a light, steady chirping sound with the bells.

4. When the children are ready, they can act out the story. You can tell those with speaking parts what to say. By the end of the story, there will be a lot of loud chirping—and laughter.

5. Collect the bell bracelets.

Questions to Ask

- Why does the mouse wake up?
- Why doesn't the first cricket stop chirping when she asks him to?
- When the mouse complains, "I asked you to stop the music. You are giving me more!" what do the crickets think she says? What do they do?
- Why is the chirping so loud at the end?

Discoveries to Make

- The force of many individual bell bracelets jingling together adds up to a much greater force.
- Greater force produces a louder sound, in the context of playing musical instruments.

> ### KEEP THE LEARNING GOING!
>
> Children may be interested in discussing other big sounds that are made up of many small forces producing sound at the same time. Examples could include leaves shaking in a strong wind, choruses of singers, horses galloping together, and even blocks being shaken out on the floor.

SHAKERS NEAR AND FAR

We've explored the relationship between force and loudness in "Clapping Loudly and Softly" and other activities. But another factor affects how our ears perceive loudness: distance. Shakers are perfect for this activity because their sound is relatively bright and easy to hear from a distance. Also, the difference in loudness between faraway and nearby shakers is dramatic and obvious.

What You'll Need

2 shakers

Activity to Try

1. Tell the children that they'll be exploring the sound of shakers that are near and shakers that are far away. Bring out the two shakers and ask for two volunteers.
2. Ask one of the volunteers to take a shaker to the middle of the circle and the other to take a shaker and find a spot that's far from the circle.
3. Ask the children in the circle to listen carefully. Have the child in the middle shake her shaker. Then have the faraway child shake his. You could repeat this a few more times if more children want turns.

Questions to Ask

- Did the shakers sound different or the same?

- How did they sound different?

- Do you think the shakers would sound even louder if they were shaken right next to your ear? If children aren't sure, try it out. Have a child shake a shaker next to each child's ear.

- Do you think they'd sound even softer if someone shook them across the street?

- Why do you think the shaker in the middle of the circle sounded louder than the shaker far outside the circle?

- As sound moves out through the air, do you think it gets softer or louder?

> **TIP**
>
> If you still have the shakers with different fillings from the "Inside the Shaker" activity, try the near-and-far exploration with them. Children can find out if all of the shakers are louder when close and softer when farther away.

Discoveries to Make

- Sounds made by nearby shakers are louder than sounds made by shakers that are far away. This is an example of a proportional relationship, illustrating the crosscutting concepts of scale, proportion, and quantity.

- Sound gets softer, or weaker, as it travels through the air.

PAPER BIRDS, PART 1

The inspiration for this activity is a kinetic sculpture by Arthur Ganson, which I saw when I visited the MIT Museum a few years ago. Pieces of folded paper "flew" and flapped as they moved individually in a mechanical flock. The piece combines science, art, sound, and motion in an oddly enchanting way. (Here's the link: https://www.youtube.com/watch?v=PGHonvREHVU.)

This activity illustrates the relationship between sound and distance, as in the "Shakers Near and Far" activity, but like Ganson's sculpture, it also involves art and movement.

What You'll Need

Paper

Scissors

Crayons and markers

Tape

Unsharpened pencils, one per child

Activity to Try

Ahead of Time:

1. Prepare the paper. Copy paper is fine, but medium to heavyweight art paper is sturdier and makes a nice flapping sound. Fold each sheet in half crosswise.

2. Draw a bird shape on each folded sheet, like the template. Take up as much of the area of the paper as you can.

3. Cut out the bird shape from one piece of paper, and color it.

4. Poke the tip of an unsharpened pencil through the center of the bird's folded edge. This will be your example to show the children.

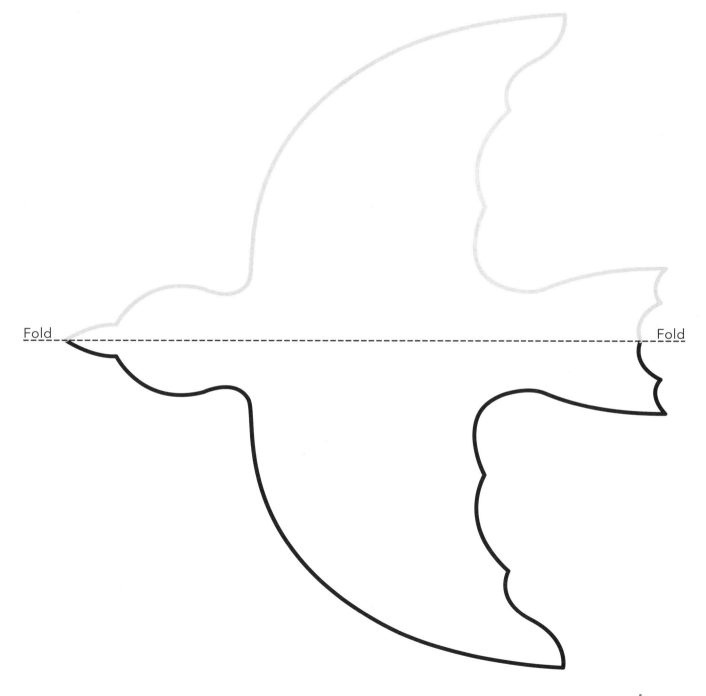

Fold   Fold

With the Children:

1. Bring out your paper bird. Show the children how your bird can fly and flap its wings. Tell them that they're going to make their own birds and explore how the birds sound up close and from far away.

2. Each child can have a turn to make the bird flap and fly. Tell them they can make the bird fly any way they want, but they need to be gentle. Ask them what they think would happen if they played with the bird too hard.

3. Put the materials out on tables. During the day, the children can create their birds. They should start by cutting out the birds on the papers you've prepared.

4. They can decorate both sides of the birds. Birds may be realistic-looking or imaginary, whatever they'd like.

5. The children may need help to poke the top half inch of the pencil through the folded edge at the top of the bird.

6. You can reinforce the bird by taping the pencil to the paper on the underside.

7. Tell the children they can name their birds if they want.

PAPER BIRDS, PART 2

When each of the children has made a paper bird, you will be ready for the next part of the activity.

Activity to Try

1. Ask the children to bring their paper birds and sit in a circle.

2. Have them take turns showing their birds to the group, describing how they colored them and sharing the names of the birds, if they wish. This is to acknowledge each student's individuality and artistic work.

3. Tell them that you're going to have two sets of birds. Have half the children take their birds to the farthest point in the room. The others should put their birds on a table for the moment. The children without birds can lie down on the carpet, facedown, so they don't peek.

4. Explain that the children with the birds will flap them up and down as they slowly "fly" them over to where the others are lying down.

5. Tell the lying-down children to raise their hands when they think the birds have arrived in the circle area. Remind the children with the birds to walk very quietly (you might want to have them take off their shoes). Everyone should be very quiet, so they can hear the birds flapping.

6. Have the "birds" slowly walk over.

7. Let the two groups switch so everyone has a chance to be both a "bird" and a "listener."

Questions to Ask

- How could you tell when the birds were close?
- What if the birds didn't flap? Do you think you'd still hear them? Why or why not? Children may want to try this.
- When the birds flap, where's the sound coming from?
- Were the birds louder when they were far away or when they were close?
- When a sound comes closer to you, is it louder or softer? Why?

> **TIP**
>
> You can expand children's thinking by asking open-ended questions, such as "What are some other things you can hear getting louder as they get closer?" and "What are some other animals that make sounds by flapping their wings?"

Discovery to Make

Children can use information from the two explorations—"Shakers Near and Far" and "Paper Birds"—to generalize that sounds are louder when they're closer and softer when they're farther away.

 # WALKING THROUGH THE JUNGLE

When I was a kid, my parents read a lot of newspapers but weren't really into disposing of them in a timely manner. So my siblings and I always had plenty of old newspapers (also known as art supplies). One of our favorite projects was making newspaper trees, which inspired this activity. Note: You may wish to split this activity into two parts: first make the trees, then create a jungle.

What You'll Need

Newspaper—four full sheets per child

Tape

Dry-erase easel or large paper and marker

Recording of instrumental African music, such as "West African Soukous" by All Star African Drum Ensemble, "African Djembe Drums" by Various Artists, "Steel Congo" by Louie Vega, or "Ghana' E" by Willie Colon (This isn't instrumental, but it's very fun dance music that children really like.)

Activity to Try

1. Ask the class if they remember the ways they've made sounds with paper, and listen to their responses. Tell them that you're going to make a new kind of sound with paper. Explain that paper comes from trees. Today, you're going to make pretend trees out of paper!

2. Give each child four sheets of newspaper. The group may need to spread out a bit, because each child will be placing her sheets flat on the floor, vertically.

3. Show the children how to roll up the newspapers from bottom to top loosely, so the resulting tube is about 4 inches in diameter. Children should hold the tubes while you go around and attach tape in three or four places, to the lowest ten inches of each tube, to hold it together.

4. Show the children how to make rips in the tops of the tubes, about six inches long, and three fingers apart.

5. They should gently bend the "leaves" outward, loosely, like a palm tree.

6. Now, the children can plant their trees in a pretend jungle! Ask ten children to go to the middle of the circle and form two rows facing each other, with a two-foot aisle between them. Have them hold the trees so that they're standing upright on the floor. (Children will need to kneel or squat.)

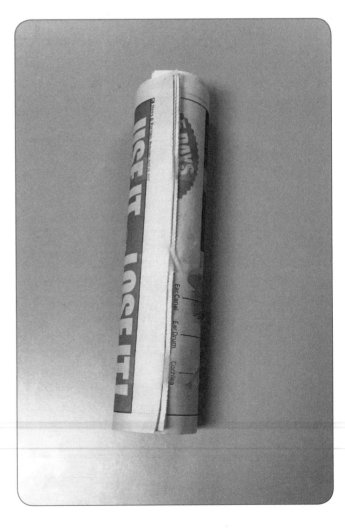

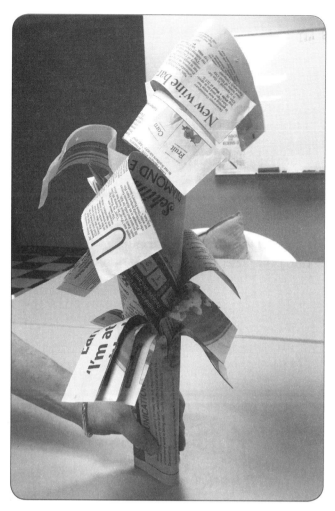

7. The remaining children can leave their trees in their spots—they're going to be walking through the jungle. Tell the children that this jungle is just starting to grow.

8. Start the music. Have the walkers hold hands as they walk slowly and carefully through the jungle. Ask the tree holders to sway their trees slightly, as in a soft breeze. The walkers can go around and back through the jungle a few more times.

9. Pause the music. Tell the children to pretend the trees have grown much taller and they've grown bigger branches. Show the children how to make the trees "grow." Very gently, pull up on the top of the tree. It will expand upward and outward by several inches. Ask the tree holders to stand up and hold the trees so the tops are at about the height of their heads.

10. Ask the children what would happen on a windy day, with these taller trees waving and shaking their branches right next to the walkers' heads. How do they think it would sound if they walked through the jungle then?

11. Start the music again, and the walkers can go through this taller, windier jungle.

12. Repeat until everyone has had a turn to be both a "tree" and a walker.

TIP

Just for fun, you could wave one of the "trees" as a signal to get children's attention throughout the day.

Questions to Ask

- You went on two jungle walks—one with little trees and one with tall trees waving in the wind. How were the walks the same?
- How were the walks different?
- You might want to set up a T-chart for their responses, like this:

WALK THROUGH LITTLE TREES	WALK THROUGH TALL TREES
Easy to walk through	Harder to walk through
Quiet	Loud
Kind of boring	Fun
Not like a real jungle	More like a real jungle

- Why do you think the second walk sounded louder?

Discovery to Make

Even nearby sounds are louder when they're right next to your ears.

STOMPING IN THE STREET

Children like this game because they think it's silly, and they're right! It's also an effective way to strengthen their learning about sounds being louder when closer and softer when farther away. With this activity, they express their knowledge in movement. Their stomping feet get softer as the elephants in the chant stomp farther away.

What You'll Need

Drum or tambourine

Activity to Try

1. Children should be standing in a circle. Tell them that this movement game is about elephants. Let them show you how they can stomp like elephants. (Young children are really great at this!)
2. Explain the game. You're going to tell a story in a chanting rhyme. At first, the elephants are going to be stomping in the street, right outside—so they're going to be very loud. Then they're going to start stomping away, down the street. Ask the children if the elephants will sound softer or louder as they get farther away.

3. Explain that at the end of the chant, the elephants will be very far away. Ask the children how that would sound.

4. Start the game by having children stomp loudly while you keep the beat with a drum or tambourine. Chant or sing the following to the tune of "Skip to My Lou":

> I woke up, in the middle of the night.
>
> I heard some elephants stomping outside!
>
> They were stomping, stomping, (stomp loudly)
>
> Stomping in the street!
>
> Stomping, stomping,
>
> Stomping in the street!
>
> They stomped and they stomped, but they did not stay.
>
> After a while they stomped away.
>
> They were stomping, stomping, (stomp more quietly)
>
> Stomping down the street!
>
> They were stomping, stomping,
>
> Stomping down the street!
>
> And even when I woke up, early the next day, (Whisper or sing very softly)
>
> I could still hear the elephants, far, far away!
>
> They were stomping, stomping, (stomp very softly)
>
> Way down the street!
>
> They were stomping, stomping,
>
> Way down the street!

5. After the game, have the children sit down.

Questions to Ask

- Can you tell me how you made the loud stomping sounds?
- How did you make the soft stomping sounds?
- This song is about elephants sounding softer as they move farther away. But we didn't move farther away. What did we do instead to show that the elephants sounded softer? If the children say, "We

stomped softer," you can lead them to the correct terminology by saying something like, "That's right. We stomped softer. We used less . . ." to help them remember the word *force*.

Discovery to Make

Children can express in movement and in language that there are two ways of making a sound become softer: by moving farther away from the listener and by using less force.

KEEP THE LEARNING GOING!

Children can invent their own versions of this game by substituting other animals for the elephants—for example, ducks waddling, horses galloping, or kangaroos jumping.

BUNNIES AND BEARS

You're packing a lot of concepts and skills into this whimsical game. The drummer needs to make loud and soft sounds by playing with different amounts of force. The "bunnies" and "bears" need to use listening skills to concentrate on hearing the loud and soft sounds. They also need the motor skills to express what they hear through movement.

What You'll Need

Drum or tambourine

Activity to Try

1. Children should be standing in a circle. Tell the group that they're going to play a game in which they'll pretend to be bunnies and bears. Ask if they can show you how a bunny hops. Then ask them to stomp their feet like a bear stomping through the woods on his hind legs.

TIP

Don't rush! Critical thinking takes time. If a child has trouble articulating a response, give him time to think it out. Don't rush in to answer for him or to interpret what you think he is trying to say. First of all, you might be wrong, and secondly, children may get the message that they're not thinking well enough or fast enough. Listening patiently shows that you value their thinking skills.

2. Bring out the drum. Tell the children that if you play loudly, they should stomp like bears. When you stop, they have to stop and freeze. Practice by playing a loud, steady beat, and have the children stomp until you stop and they freeze.

3. Tell them that if you play softly, they should hop like bunnies. When you stop, they have to stop and freeze. Practice by playing a very soft beat, and have them hop like bunnies until you stop and they freeze.

4. Pass the drum to the child on your left and let her play a beat. Tell her that she can play either loudly or softly, and the other children will be bunnies or bears depending on the kind of sound they hear.

5. Continue until each child has had a turn to play the drum or tambourine.

Questions to Ask

- What are some other ways we could move to show that we hear loud sounds?
- What are some other ways we could move to show that we hear soft sounds?
- How did you know when to be a bear or a bunny? Did someone tell you in words?

Discoveries to Make

- Children can use movement to show that they hear loud or soft sounds.
- It takes more force to make loud sounds than soft sounds.

CHAPTER FIVE

FAST AND SLOW SOUNDS: THE SCIENCE OF SPEED AND TEMPO

Ask the children if they remember when they felt their heartbeats. Tell them that we measure how fast or slow a heartbeat is by counting how many beats are in a minute. That's the same way we measure something called tempo in music. Ask the children if they've ever heard the word *tempo*, and if they know what it means. Listen to their responses with interest but no evaluation.

KEY CONCEPT

The more time there is between beats, the slower the tempo will be.

Explain that *tempo* is the speed of a piece of music. The tempo tells us how slow or fast the music is, but tempo is more than just speed. Tempo tells us how many beats the music has in a minute. Tempo is also called *beats per minute*. Ask the children to hold one hand up in the air. (Hold your arm up in front of you.) Then ask them to bring it down fast. (Do this with the children.) Explain that though the movement was fast and had a fast speed, it didn't have a tempo, because it didn't have a beat.

Ask the children to listen while you pat your legs. Pat your thighs in a fairly fast, steady beat. Ask the children to describe the tempo. Then, invite them to show you how they would pat their legs in a slow tempo. Have the children use fast and slow tempos for clapping, patting their shoulders, and other movements that the children suggest.

Ask the children, "These sounds had tempos, because they had . . . ?" Children should remember that sounds have tempos only if they have beats. Tell the children that they'll be learning more about beats and tempos and how different tempos make music sound different.

THE SPEED AND TEMPO OF A BEACH BALL

Tempo is a special kind of speed. Every movement has speed, but only movement with a steady beat, or pulse, has a tempo. That's why in this activity we bring the children back to feeling their heartbeats.

Tempo is all about the beat. Like the heartbeat, tempo is measured in beats per minute. So once again, understanding a musical concept starts with our first musical experience—the heartbeat. Then you'll move on to an object that can demonstrate two kinds of speed, both with and without a tempo: a beach ball. Leading this activity is exciting, because you can really see the wheels turning in the children's minds as they grapple with the problem of how to create a tempo with the beach ball.

What You'll Need

Sturdy beach ball, not too big

Stethoscope (optional)

Large bag

Activity to Try

1. Have the beach ball in a closed bag next to you. Ask the children to feel their heartbeats. Lay your right palm flat on your chest, a little left of center. Then, lay your left palm on top to remind them how to feel their heartbeats. If they're having trouble, you can bring out the stethoscope again—children always love it. After they can all feel their heartbeats, they can rest their hands in their laps again.

2. Tell the children that the heartbeat is like the tempo of their body. *Tempo* is a special kind of speed—it's the speed of beats. Hearts have a beat and so does music. But if a movement doesn't have a beat, it doesn't have a tempo.

3. Bring out the beach ball. Choose two children sitting across the circle from each other, and have them roll the ball back and forth.

4. Choose two other children and ask them to roll the ball a little faster.

5. Finally, have two children roll the ball to each other very slowly.

6. Tell the children that they rolled the ball at a medium speed, a fast speed, and a slow speed. Every time the ball rolled, it had a certain speed. Ask the children if it had a tempo. Students should be able to tell you that the rolling ball did not have a tempo because it did not have a beat.

7. Ask the class if they can think of any way to make the ball have a tempo. If they're really stuck, you can lead them by asking, "What can we do with a ball that has a beat?" But give them time to think—sometimes it takes a while for children to realize that bouncing a ball has a beat, which will make it have a tempo.

8. When someone suggests bouncing, have them demonstrate bouncing the ball. They may need to move to an uncarpeted area. Then, ask the children if they could hear the beat of the bouncing ball.

Exploring the Science of Sounds: 100 Musical Activities for Young Children

Questions to Ask

- What did we do with the ball that had a speed but no tempo?
- Do you remember about cause and effect—that everything that happens has a cause that made it happen? What happened to the ball to make it have a tempo? What did you do to it?
- Why did bouncing the ball have a tempo?

Discoveries to Make

- The sound of a rolling ball has a speed but does not have a tempo, because it does not have a beat.
- The sound of a bouncing ball has a tempo, because it has a beat.
- This activity supported the critical-thinking skill of classifying, based on children's careful listening to different kinds of sounds.
- This activity also reinforced the crosscutting concept of cause and effect.

> ### KEEP THE LEARNING GOING!
>
> Ask the children for another idea for moving the ball in a way that has a speed but no tempo. Give them time to come up with throwing. Ask them for other ways to move the ball that will have a tempo. They might suggest patting the ball or tapping it rhythmically against another object.

NAMES BETWEEN BEATS

Have you ever noticed how your ears perk up when you hear your name? Even in a crowd of people, if you hear your own first name spoken, your attention zooms right to it. You can't help it. Young children also have this seemingly magnetic attraction to the sound of their own names. Including children's names makes any activity more interesting and engaging. And in this exploration, names aren't just attention getting—they're an integral part of the activity.

What You'll Need

No materials needed

Activity to Try

1. Tell the children that you're going to see how to make a tempo slower by lengthening the time between beats. Tell them you'll do this by using their names.

2. Start with the name of the child on your right. Invite the class to help you get the beat going by clapping and chanting his name. Clap and chant, "(Clap) Brycen (Clap) Brycen (Clap) Brycen (Clap) Brycen" and so on. Do this at a pretty brisk pace.

3. Tell the children to add the name of the next child in the circle: "(Clap) BrycenMcKenzie (Clap) BrycenMcKenzie" and so on.

4. Ask the class if the beat stayed the same or if it was different. They may say it was slower or longer or took more time. These are all good answers. The important thing is that they hear that there's more time between beats.

5. Add the next child's name: "(Clap) BrycenMcKenzieEva (Clap) BrycenMcKenzieEva" and so on.

6. Continue until you get to five or six names, or until it gets too tongue-twisty.

7. Repeat the game until everyone has heard his name. It may seem tedious, but including all the children in the activity will make it more engaging and memorable for all of them.

Questions to Ask

- When we added more names between beats, did the tempo get slower or faster?
- When we added more names between the beats, was there less time or more time between beats?
- How did we make the tempo slower?

Discovery to Make

Adding more time between beats makes the tempo slower.

When children are familiar with this activity, you can try adding names for a while and then subtracting them, one at a time, to make the tempo faster. Children are familiar with adding and subtracting objects (visual learning). Using the words *add* and *subtract* in this context gives children a new modality–hearing–to understand these words.

MOVING THE DRUMS

Although the ability to perceive the beat in music is a fundamental brain process that develops unconsciously (University of Amsterdam, 2016), the concepts of beat and tempo are fairly abstract. This is why I like to help children begin to explore this territory by using the concrete examples of heartbeats and beach balls and the familiar sounds of their names. This activity is concrete, too, as children watch the physical distance between the drums increase.

What You'll Need

2 drums with large, flat heads or 2 tambourines

Activity to Try

1. Ask the children if they remember how they made a tempo slower. Listen to their responses.

2. Explain that now you're going to make a tempo slower by adding more time between beats again but in a different way. Place the drums on the floor in front of you.

3. Start playing the left drum with your left hand and then the right drum with your right hand, over and over, to make a steady, fairly fast tempo. Ask the children how they'd describe this tempo.

4. Choose a child to play the drums, and set him up in the middle of the circle, with plenty of room on his left and right sides. After he's played the fast tempo for a while, thank him and ask him to stay there.

5. Ask the children what they think will happen if you move the drums farther apart. Will his tempo get faster or slower, or will it stay the same? Listen to any responses.

6. Move the drums about six inches farther apart, and ask the child to play the beat again. (It helps to have one child hold each drum in place while he's playing–the instruments tend to slide on some surfaces.) Chances are he'll be able to keep the beat at pretty much the same tempo.

7. Continue to move the drums farther apart. The child will have to play at a slower tempo as he struggles to reach both drums.

8. Ask if anything is happening to the tempo. By now most children will know that the tempo is getting slower.

Questions to Ask

- Why did the tempo get slower? Children will answer this question in many ways. They may say, "He couldn't reach the drums," or "The drums got too far apart." These are good answers—they show that the children are thinking through this.

- When we moved the drums, was there more time between beats? If they're unsure, have your drummer play a condensed version of the activity, so the group can listen carefully to the tempo with the drums close together and with them very far apart. With this stark contrast, most children will reflect on their previous opinions and understand that when the drums were farther apart, there was more time between beats.

- How did moving the drums make the tempo slower?

Discoveries to Make

- Increasing the physical distance between two instruments is another way to slow a tempo being played on both of those instruments.

- This activity also reinforces the children's knowledge that when there is more time between beats, the tempo will be slower.

> **TIP**
>
> Although it's more accessible and understandable to start with the drums close together and watch them get farther apart, it's a fact of life that for young children, getting faster is more fun than getting slower. Try doing the activity again in reverse, giving another child a chance to play the drums. Begin with the drums far apart, and gradually bring them closer together, making the tempo faster.

"T-E-M-P-O"

While the concept of tempo—the idea that tempo is a kind of speed that has a beat—is still fresh in their minds, this game (based on the song "B-I-N-G-O") will help children review that knowledge. It will also give them a chance to demonstrate that knowledge by changing the tempo of their singing.

What You'll Need

No materials needed

Activity to Try

1. Teach the children this song about tempo, sung to the tune of "B-I-N-G-O":

> *There is a word that's all about*
>
> *How fast a beat is moving.*
>
> *T-E-M-P-O, T-E-M-P-O,*
>
> *T-E-M-P-O, and tempo is its name-o.*

2. Clap to the beat while singing.
3. Ask if anyone can show you a way to clap in a slow tempo. Have a child demonstrate a slow tempo, and then ask the class to join in the slow-tempo clapping. Finally, clap while singing the song in the slow tempo.
4. Do the same with a fast tempo—and a super-fast tempo. That's always popular!

Questions to Ask

- We sang the song in four different tempos. Can you tell me what they were?
- How did we show the beat in each different tempo?
- Do songs have to be in one tempo all the time, or can we change the tempo? If yes, how?

Discovery to Make

Children can sing a song in several different tempos.

KEEP THE LEARNING GOING!

Reintroducing this song every few weeks is a fun and effective way to help your students review the concept of tempo.

METRONOME TEMPOS

I don't have very fond memories of metronomes from my childhood piano-lesson days. Once in a while my teacher would have me practice pieces with the strict tick-tock of an old-fashioned mechanical metronome to keep my tempo from wandering. Its relentless, monotonous ticking was effective but a little too regimented for my taste.

As an early-childhood music teacher, though, I've come to appreciate the value of metronomes. They take the fuzzy idea of "beats per minute" and make it more real and accessible for young children. In fact, my students are always fascinated by metronome tempos and love to listen to the different numbers of beats per minute.

What You'll Need

Any kind of metronome

Activity to Try

1. Place the metronome in front of you. (I use the one that's built into my electronic keyboard. These sometimes have a moving hand-clapping icon to show you how to follow the beat. There are also several inexpensive or free metronome apps for smartphones, as well as free online metronomes.) Tell the children that one way to show how slow or fast a piece of music should be is with a *metronome*. Explain that your keyboard, computer, or phone has a built-in metronome. A slow tempo will have about 60 beats per minute or fewer. Set your metronome to 60 beats per minute and let the children listen to the tempo. A fast tempo will have at least 120 beats per minute and a very fast tempo, about 190 beats per minute (let the children listen to these settings).

2. Remind the children that both heartbeats and musical tempos are measured in beats per minute, which means how many beats are in one minute.

3. Have the children try singing the alphabet song at each of these different tempos, to hear how it sounds. (The alphabet song is a particularly good song to use for this exploration because you can start by singing one letter per beat, which makes it easier for everyone to stay together.) Have the class sing the song with you at the three tempos. It helps children stay on tempo if you all clap to the beat while you sing.

Questions to Ask

• Do you remember what the numbers of the tempos mean?

• (You might give a hint, such as "The numbers mean how many beats are in a . . .")

• Did it feel different to sing the song at the three different tempos?

• When there's a low number of beats in a minute, will that tempo be fast or slow?

• When there's a high number of beats in a minute, will that tempo be fast or slow?

Discovery to Make

Low tempos have fewer beats per minute, and faster tempos have more beats per minute.

KEEP THE LEARNING GOING!

You and the children can clap a beat and find out what the tempo is. Looking at a watch or clock with a second hand, have the class clap a beat with you and count on every clap. Stop when you reach the one-minute mark and tell them how many beats you all clapped—that was your tempo. But be prepared—they'll almost always want to try it again to see if they can get a faster tempo!

ANIMAL HEARTBEATS

By pre-kindergarten, most children have a strong base of knowledge about animals. They know the appearance, sounds, movements, and size of many different animals. This activity builds on that knowledge to relate the size of various animals to their heartbeats (their "tempos") in a fun and developmentally appropriate way.

What You'll Need

A metronome

Activity to Try

1. Place the metronome (you'll need one that can play from seven to 205 bpm—a good free one online is webMetronome at http://www.webmetronome.com) in front of you. Remind the children that the heartbeat is the tempo of the body, and tell them that you're going to learn about the heartbeats of different animals.

2. Remind the children that heartbeats and tempos are both measured by how many beats are in one minute. Tell them that you looked up the tempos of some animal heartbeats for them to listen to.

3. Tell the children you're going to hear the tempo of a whale's heartbeat. Set the metronome at seven bpm and play it for the group. This is ridiculously slow (there are almost nine seconds between beats).

4. Ask the children to describe the tempo. Listen to their responses.

5. Play the tempo of a bear's heartbeat by setting the metronome at 40 bpm. Again, ask the children to describe the beat and listen to their answers. Continue with the tempos of a large dog (85 bpm) and a cat (130 bpm). Ask them whether they think a small rabbit's heartbeat would be faster or slower than the cat's. When they've reached a consensus, play the rabbit's heartbeat (205 bpm). Ask them if their prediction was correct.

6. Then tell the children they're going to pretend to walk like animals. If there's room in the circle area for all of your students to walk around without bumping into each other, have them all participate. Otherwise, choose three or four children to be bears. They can slowly walk around inside the circle like bears while the class sings "The Bears Went Over the Mountain" (plural style):

> *The bears went over the mountain,*
> *The bears went over the mountain,*
> *The bears went over the mountain,*
> *To see what they could see.*

7. Notice I'm not suggesting children walk to the heartbeat tempos, which are quite a bit slower than most walking (or hopping) tempos. But animals' walking tempos, like their heartbeats, do generally correspond to their sizes.

8. Continue with dogs, cats, and rabbits going over the mountain—each a little faster.

Questions to Ask

- How did it feel to walk like a bear? Was it slower or faster than the way you usually walk?
- How fast do you think the tempo of a mouse's heartbeat would be?
- (A mouse's heart beats at 670 bpm—faster than any metronome I could find!)
- Do all animals' heartbeats have the same tempo?

Discovery to Make

The heartbeat of every kind of animal has its own tempo.

TIP

If someone asks why smaller animals have faster heartbeats, explain that the heart pumps blood for the body to use. Generally, smaller animals have smaller hearts, and it takes less time for blood to go through a small heart than a larger one.

Exploring the Science of Sounds: 100 Musical Activities for Young Children

"THE TORTOISE AND THE HARE"

"The Tortoise and the Hare" is one of those classic music-teacher stories for teaching about fast and slow sounds. Children love laughing at the lazy, thinks-he's-so-great hare and rooting for the quiet, plodding tortoise; this old tale is always a hit. I've used it, adding short musical interludes for the children to move fast or slowly, but I've felt frustrated when some students seemed to disregard the musical part of the interludes. During the hare's rare bursts of energy, these children would just move, not with the tempo of the song, but as fast as they could (Which is really, really fast and for some reason, always involves screaming!).

Since I've worked with children on the concept of tempo, however, I've found it's much easier for them to follow along in a rhythmic way. And it's more fun for everyone when the whole group is singing and keeping the beat together.

What You'll Need

A copy of "The Tortoise and the Hare"

Activity to Try

1. Show the class the cover of "The Tortoise and the Hare." (Many excellent versions are out there; my favorite is by Janet Stevens. It's very funny and clever.)

2. Ask the children whether they've heard this story. (Usually some have, and it's better to hear their comments now, rather than while you're reading the story!)

3. Talk about tortoises with the children. From the cover, they'll see that the tortoise looks like a turtle. Ask them whether they know how turtles move—if they're fast or slow.

4. Talk about how the hare (who is like a rabbit) would move. If children want to tell you (briefly!) about their experiences seeing a turtle or a rabbit, allowing this will be empowering for them and helpful for the other children who might not have seen these animals.

5. Tell the group that in this story, the tortoise and the hare are in a race. Tell them they'll sing fast during the hare's parts, and slowly for the tortoise. Sing the tortoise's song (to the tune of "The Wheels on the Bus," but very slowly and sluggishly):

> *The tortoise likes to go so slow, slow, slow,*
> *Slow, slow, slow,*
> *Slow, slow, slow,*
> *The tortoise likes to go so slow, slow, slow,*
> *That's how he goes.*

6. Explain that you're also going to move to the beat of the song. Have them remain seated and pat their thighs slowly, alternating left and right hands, as if their hands are walking. Rehearse the song with the walking movements, at a nice, slow tempo.

7. Sing the hare's song at a fast tempo:

> *The hare likes to run so fast, fast, fast,*
> *Fast, fast, fast,*
> *Fast, fast, fast,*
> *The hare likes to run so fast, fast, fast,*
> *That's how he runs.*

8. Again, have the children sing along while patting their thighs, but this time to the fast tempo.

9. Read the story and have the children join in the song when the slow, slow tortoise and the fast hare move.

Questions to Ask

- Was it hard to keep the fast tempo with your hands?
- How many thought it was actually harder to go slowly? (Doing anything slowly is tough for some children.)
- Was it fun to sing and move slowly and fast like the tortoise and the hare? Did it make the story more exciting?

Discovery to Make

Adding music and movement at different tempos can add excitement to a story.

> **TIP**
>
> Just to sneak in a little more science, you might want to bring in pictures of a real tortoise and hare. Children can discuss how these animals are similar to turtles and rabbits, and how they're different.

PARTNER CLAPPING

In the tempo section's activities, we've played with beach balls, sung songs, we've walked, patted our thighs, and clapped our hands, to learn and experience different tempos. Now you're going to use this learning to play a fun, but tricky, game. You're adding the challenge of coordinating your movements with those of a partner. This involves cooperation, self-regulation, eye-hand coordination, and usually, lots of giggling!

What You'll Need

2 rhythm sticks

Activity to Try

1. Tell the class that in this game you're going to clap to slow and fast tempos, but you're not going to be clapping your own hands. Explain that each child will clap with a partner.

2. Ask the child on your right to help you demonstrate how to play this game. Face the child and hold your hands up, palms facing out, pat-a-cake style. Have the child hold their hands the same way. Tell the children you're going to start with a slow tempo. Chant "Clap–clap–clap–clap" and so on at a slow pace, while you clap the child's hands. After a while, try a fast tempo.

3. Pair the children with partners, going around the circle. Have partners face each other. Then bring out the rhythm sticks. Tell the group you're going to start tapping a slow tempo for them to clap, the way you did with your helper.

4. Begin tapping at a slow tempo. If the children are doing well, go straight to a fast tempo, and then switch tempos. If you think they need a little help, you can chant "Clap–clap–clap–clap" for the first fifteen seconds or so.

> **TIP**
>
> If children are getting a little overenthusiastic about clapping fast, without really following the tempo you're playing, stop. Gently lead them back to clapping at the tempo with suggestions, such as "I'm watching to see who's clapping right with the beat. Oh, I see Kyung-Soon and Elijah are clapping at the right tempo," and "It's really hard to clap right on the beat when the tempo is fast. Let's try it again."

Questions to Ask

- Is it harder to clap with a partner or by yourself?
- Was it easier to clap to a slow tempo or to a fast tempo?
- How did you know which tempo to clap?

Discoveries to Make

- Children can coordinate their movements to a musical tempo.
- Children can coordinate their movements with those of a partner.

SLOW AND FAST BODY SOUNDS

You're revisiting the sounds we can make with our bodies in this activity. Now it's time to find out if you can make various body sounds at a fast tempo. Some of them aren't so easy! But children still have fun trying.

What You'll Need

No materials needed

Activity to Try

1. Remind the class that they've explored the sounds they can make with their bodies. Tell them that you're going to play a singing game with some of those sounds, and new ones, too. Tell them you'll be making these sounds at slow and fast tempos. Really fast tempos! (I always say that because they love fast so much.)

2. Introduce the song by explaining that they need to follow your tempo. To do that, they'll have to listen carefully and watch you as you keep the beat. Tell them that first you're going to clap your hands. Clap your hands to the beat as you start at a slow tempo (to the tune of "Down by the Bay"):

> *My hands clap slow, my hands clap slow,*
>
> *They clap as slow as they can go,*
>
> (Then change to a quick tempo)
>
> *Then they clap fast, they clap so fast,*
>
> *They are really, really, fast,*
>
> *Really, really, fast,*
>
> *Fast, fast, fast, fast!*

3. You may sing these additional verses:

> *My feet stomp slow . . .* (Staying seated, children can stomp their feet in front of them)
>
> *My fingers tap slow . . .* (Children should tap pointer fingers together like rhythm sticks)
>
> *My hands pat slow . . .* (Children should pat knees)
>
> *My elbows knock slow . . .* (Children should knock elbows together)
>
> *My knees knock slow . . .* (Children should knock knees together)
>
> *My hands clap slow . . .* (Children should hold hands far apart, one high and one low, and clap together—this is very hard to do fast!)
>
> *My feet tap slow . . .* (Children should hold legs out straight in front with feet flexed and tap feet together—this is also hard to do fast.)

4. Ask the children to suggest ideas, too. (Avoid using the head in this activity—children may shake their heads too hard, which can be harmful.)

Questions to Ask

- Was it easy to stomp your feet really fast?
- What about knocking your knees together? Was that easy to do at a fast tempo?
- What was the hardest sound to make at a fast tempo?
- Why do you think it was harder to make some of the sounds really fast?

Discoveries to Make

- Children can make many different sounds with their bodies at slow and fast tempos.
- Some parts of the body can't move very fast, or in certain ways, because of their size, their shape, or the way their bones move at the joints. This relates to structure and function, one of the crosscutting concepts that apply to all domains of science.

KEEP THE LEARNING GOING!

You can use this activity during transitions for the rest of the day. For instance, ask the children to sing the song using a sound they can make with their fingers, their knuckles, or their heels.

FROGS AND LILY PADS

Jumping like a frog is always fun—and it's a great workout in this activity, since children are jumping in and out of "lily pads," adding some locomotor movement into the mix. Listening skills get a workout too, as students need to respond not only to the "hopping tempo," but also to an occasional pause in the music.

What You'll Need

A recording of brisk, cheerful "hopping music"

My favorite: "Pine Apple Rag" by Scott Joplin

Masking tape

Activity to Try

1. Children should be sitting in a circle. While they're sitting, use the masking tape to make two or three large "lily pads" on the floor, within the circle. (You can find lily pad shapes online to copy.) There should be enough total space in the lily pads for all the students to fit fairly comfortably.

2. To keep them engaged while you're setting up the lily pads, ask the children if they can guess what you're doing, and respond to their guesses as you go along with, "Maybe," "Hmm," and other noncommittal replies.

3. When you're done, tell the class that you're going to pretend to be jumping frogs, and the shapes on the floor are lily pads.

4. Show the children how frogs jump. Be sure everyone is jumping up from a squatting position. This isn't just "frogly" correctness—it requires more energy and coordination than regular jumping, and helps those little muscles get strong. Let them jump in place a few times.

5. Tell them that when the music starts, they should listen to the beat and frog-jump in place. (Children may need to spread out a bit to have room for jumping without bumping.) Explain that when the music stops, that means they need to jump over to one of the lily pads! When it starts again, they should jump back to their places. And so on.

6. Start the music and begin. Two minutes is usually plenty—this activity is fun, but tiring!

Questions to Ask

- Did you feel that this tempo was slow or fast?
- Would it be easier to jump along to a faster tempo? How about a slower one? (If they're not sure, try it and see. Clap out a very fast tempo, and a slow one, for them to jump to. They may revise their original opinions when they actually try this out.)
- Which was easier—when you were jumping at whatever pace you wanted, before we started the music, or when you jumped to the beat of the music?

> **TIP**
>
> As a variation, play this game as "Rabbits and Rabbit Holes" in the spring.

Discovery to Make

Children can jump to the beat of a piece of music.

CHAPTER SIX
HIGH AND LOW SOUNDS: THE SCIENCE OF PITCH

(You'll need a glockenspiel.)

Pitch is the relative highness or lowness of a sound. The squeak of a mouse is an example of a high pitched sound; the growl of a tiger is a low-pitched sound. The bigger an object, the lower the pitch will be when the object is hit, blown into, plucked, or strummed. Some instruments can create multiple pitches, or tones, by the way they're played. For instance, you can press down on a guitar fret to make a string shorter and the pitch higher.

KEY CONCEPT

Bigger objects produce lower sounds than smaller objects.

Pitch is a pretty complex subject, but the core concept, that big things make low sounds and small things make high sounds, is one that young children can understand. Exploring the relationship between size and pitch can be done with touchable, audible objects, and presents many opportunities for children to question, predict, and test their ideas, and to communicate and visually represent what they learn.

A glockenspiel is an excellent tool to kick off this discussion, since it's one of the few typical early-childhood classroom instruments that is pitched. Most instruments they use, such as shakers and rhythm sticks, make a sound, but not musical tones. The glockenspiel has bars, arranged from long to short, that play tones ranging from low to high. It's easy for children to see the differences in length, and to hear the differences in pitch. (Note: Although the two terms are often confused, a glockenspiel has metal bars, while a xylophone has wooden ones.) You'll be exploring the glockenspiel in more depth in a later activity about pitch, but for now it's a good introduction to thinking about high and low sounds.

Play the three highest tones on the glockenspiel a few times. Then play the three lowest tones. You might say, "Some things sound high," playing the high notes again, and "Some things sound low," playing the low notes.

Ask the class to think about high sounds for a minute—high sounding animals, people, musical instruments, or other things—without talking yet. After a while, ask if they can think of something that makes a high sound. Listen to the children's examples of high sounds. Then do the same for low sounds. If it's hard for them to think of low sounds, you could ask them if a kitten or a cow makes a low sound. They'll know the low sound of a cow mooing. You can also ask the children if babies or grown-ups have higher voices.

Children usually have a lot to say about high and low sounds they've heard. When they're finished, ask them if they've ever wondered why some sounds are high and some sounds are low. Ask them what they think might be the reason.

Listen to and acknowledge all of the children's ideas. Tell them that you're going to be exploring many high and low sounds, and finding out why they sound the way they do.

PLUCKING SMALL AND LARGE RUBBER BANDS

Like aluminum foil, a rubber band is one of those common household items grown-ups take for granted, but children see with fresh, wondering eyes. We just stuff rubber bands in the junk drawer and take them out for purely utilitarian reasons, never sensing their potential for creative play and scientific investigations. (Of course, rubber bands can snap unpredictably and should always be used with adult supervision.)

Children explored the musicality of rubber bands in the "Vibration—A Special Kind of Motion" and "Different Kinds of Stringed Instruments" activities. Now you're going to be finding out about the difference in pitch between small and large rubber bands.

What You'll Need

A large and small rubber band—The larger rubber band should also be thicker.

Square or rectangular plastic container, without lid (Both rubber bands should stretch comfortably over the container.)

Extra rubber bands of various lengths and widths

Extra containers of different sizes

Activity to Try

1. Have the extra materials off to the side in a closed bag, for children to experiment with later if they wish. Ask the group if they remember talking about high and low sounds. Go over some of the reasons they thought objects made high or low sounds, including difference in size, if children had mentioned that as a possibility.

2. Bring out the two rubber bands and show the children that you've brought a little one and a big one.

3. Explain that they're going to pluck them, as they plucked rubber bands earlier. Tell them that this time you're going to listen to the different size rubber bands being plucked, to hear if one of them makes a higher sound. Tell them the scientific and musical term for a higher sound is a higher pitch.

4. Wrap the rubber bands, side by side, around the container. Say that you're going to pass it around the circle, so everyone can pluck both rubber bands and find out if they sound the same, or if one has a lower pitch and one has a higher pitch.

5. When they've all played and listened, ask for their observations. Which rubber band sounded higher, or did they both sound the same? If some children aren't sure, let them try again.

Exploring the Science of Sounds: 100 Musical Activities for Young Children

Questions to Ask

- What if we tried this with other small and large rubber bands? Do you think a smaller one will always sound higher than a bigger one?

- Do you think it mattered how thick or thin the rubber bands were?

- How do you think we could get an even higher pitch?

- How could we get a lower pitch? (Children might suggest using rubber bands of different lengths, or of different widths. These are both right answers. Some may even suggest using different size containers, which is also correct. Try out the suggested ideas.)

TIP

If a child has a hard time distinguishing the pitches of the rubber bands, it can help if you pluck the bands near their ear.

Discoveries to Make

- A shorter, thinner rubber band made a higher sound when plucked than a longer, thicker rubber band.

- Children learned that the scientific and musical term for the highness or lowness of a sound is pitch.

PLUCKING UKELELE STRINGS USING FRETS

The principle children discovered in the "Plucking Small and Large Rubber Bands" activity, that small objects produce higher pitched sounds than larger objects, is basic to all pitched instruments. Now students will explore this principle in the context of playing a musical instrument. When you press down on a string right behind a fret (frets are the horizontal raised bars) on the neck of a ukulele or guitar, you effectively make that string shorter, producing a higher-pitched tone.

In all pitched instruments, the tones are in mathematical proportion. This proportion is very audible on the ukulele.

What You'll Need

A ukulele or guitar (the distance in pitch between the frets is the same)

Activity to Try

1. Bring out the ukulele or guitar. If you're able to play a song to sing with the class, that's a nice way to open this activity.

2. Point out the horizontal bars on the neck of the instrument. Explain that these are called frets and they do something very special.

3. Ask the children to listen closely as you pluck an open string, and then play the same string with your finger pressing on it right in back of a fret. (For a dramatic change, use the fourth or fifth fret.) Ask them to describe what they heard. Continue pressing down behind each fret for that string and plucking, so the class can hear the pitches, all the way down to the last fret.

4. They'll know that the tones are higher and higher in pitch as you press down on the string, making it shorter and shorter. Ask the children if they can guess why that happened. Ask if they observed anything else recently that produced lower and higher sounds. Encourage the children to reflect on how those things were similar to the ukulele string. The goal is not to get to the right answer as soon as possible—it's to think logically and build on their prior learning. Let them take their time wondering out loud and discussing possibilities.

5. Next, the children will get a chance to change the pitch themselves. Along with the children, count the frets. (A ukulele has twelve, a guitar has twenty.) Help a child to hold the ukulele the regular way, or to hold it flat on their lap—many children find this easier. Show them how to hold a string down right behind a fret and pluck it.

6. If you have time, let every child have a turn. If not, continue another day, because the hands-on experience is really helpful. It makes the learning more fun and engaging—and helps children retain what they've seen and heard.

Questions to Ask

- What happened to the sound when you held down a string?

- What about other instruments with strings, like a violin? Do you think their strings would also sound higher if we held them down? (If the class is divided on this, watch a video together of a violinist playing—they'll see her holding the strings down to change the pitch.)

- How was holding down the frets on the ukulele like plucking the small and large rubber bands?

Discoveries to Make

- Holding down a string on a ukulele is a way of shortening the string—making it smaller—to produce a higher-pitched tone.
- Children begin to understand the concept of proportion—that as we hold down strings near frets closer to the sound hole, making the string shorter and shorter, the pitch gets higher and higher. This relates to the crosscutting concept of scale, proportion, and quantity, which applies across all domains of science.

> Of course, another way to change the pitch of a ukulele string is to adjust the tuning peg at the end of the string, attached to the head (top) of the guitar. However, when I show children how I do this, they really want to try it themselves, and they can inadvertently cause the instrument to go out of tune very quickly. Rather than interest children in something I don't want them to do, I stick to teaching them about the use of frets.

 WILL SHORTER BARS ON A GLOCKENSPIEL SOUND HIGHER THAN LONGER BARS, EVEN IF WE TURN THE GLOCKENSPIEL AROUND?

The glockenspiel is a remarkable teaching tool—for music, math, and science. Musically, it's like a miniature piano. (And it's much nicer to listen to than the tinny, dinky sounds of a toy piano.) The eight bars of the glockenspiel play the eight notes of a musical scale—usually the same notes you'll find on the piano from middle C to high C. Mathematically, the bars are eight different sizes, from longest to shortest. Also, this instrument is a developmentally appropriate example of the scientific concept of pitch. Its notes get higher-pitched proportionately as the bars get shorter. But sometimes children confuse "longer to shorter" with "left side to right side." You'll experiment to hear what happens if the bars are turned around.

What You'll Need

A glockenspiel

2 mallets

"Write-and-wipe" type easel, or large paper and marker

Activity to Try

1. Place the glockenspiel on the floor in front of you. Tell the children that you're going to do an experiment with the bars on the glockenspiel.

2. First, talk about the bars. Play them, and ask the children which bars made the lowest sounds. Ask them which bars made the highest sounds.

3. Listen to the children's responses and confirm that bigger, or longer, things make lower sounds than smaller, or shorter, things.

4. Wonder aloud what would happen if we turned the glockenspiel around, so the short ones would be on this side (point to the bars on your left) and the longer ones on this side (point to the bars on your right)? Ask the children if they think the long bars would still sound lower than the short bars. Listen to the children's responses.

5. With the children's help, set up an experiment. Ask them what they need first for an experiment. (They'll know they need a question.) Write "Question" and write out the question ("Will longer bars always sound lower than shorter bars?") as you say it aloud.

6. Write "Hypothesis" and ask the group if they can agree on a prediction. If they do, write it down. If they don't, draw a question mark.

7. Write "Experiment" and write "Move the glockenspiel around and play it."

8. Turn the glockenspiel around. Then ask for two children to play the bars—one for the longest bars and one for the shortest ones. Have them play, one at a time.

Questions to Ask

- Did the long bars still sound lower than the short bars? Write "Results" and their answer.

- Do you think the bars would sound the same no matter where they were on the glockenspiel?

- Does the sound of each bar stay high or low, no matter which way we play the glockenspiel?

- Why does it stay high or low? (They will realize that the pitch of a sound, its highness or lowness, depends only on size. Tell the class that this is called a proportional relationship and it never changes. It's true for all sounds, all the time.)

- Do you remember another proportional relationship we learned about? (Children will remember they learned about force and loudness.)

Discoveries to Make

- Size is the only thing that makes a bar on the glockenspiel sound high or low. How the glockenspiel is turned doesn't change the pitch.
- The relationship between size and pitch is a proportional relationship that never changes, like the relationship between force and loudness.

> **KEEP THE LEARNING GOING!**
>
> If you have an electronic keyboard available, you can show children how the notes from middle C to high C are the same scale as the bars on the glockenspiel.

 THE PITCHMOBILE

Hiding in plain sight (well, inside your kitchen cabinet) is an amazing musical instrument, just sitting there waiting for the concert to begin. Its sound can be subtle or festively earsplitting, and young children love it. Yes, I'm talking about the aluminum can, the instrument that comes free with every purchase of soup.

Okay, so maybe it's more schoolyard than Juilliard, but for sheer versatility, the aluminum can has few peers. Place a few together and you've got a mini drum set. Thread a string through a hole in the bottom of a can and it's a bass. In this activity, inspired by tinkling aluminum-can wind chimes, young children experience the proportional relationship between size and pitch.

What You'll Need

Long cardboard tube

Aluminum foil or construction paper (optional)

String

At least four cans of different sizes, empty, with no lids

Hammer and nail

Duct tape

Masking tape

Mallet

Activity to Try

Ahead of Time:

Time to make a pitchmobile! (I call it that because it has graduated pitches like a glockenspiel but in a mobile-type structure.) This is easy. Really. I'm the least handy person in the world, and it took me less than an hour.

1. Thoroughly wash and dry the cans. (I used a tomato-paste can, a small soup can, a vegetable can, and a spaghetti sauce can.) The labels usually come off during the washing process, with a little extra scrubbing. When cans are dry, cover the open edge with masking tape. Then use the nail to hammer a hole in the bottom of each can.

2. If the tube has writing on it, you might want to cover it with foil or colored paper.

3. Cut the same number of pieces of string, about 18 inches long, as the number of cans. Make a large knot in the end of each piece of string. Then thread a string through the hole in each can until the can is dangling at the end.

4. Wrap the other ends of each string around the tube at regular intervals and tie knots to secure them. You may want to cover these with duct tape for more strength—young children can be pretty tough on instruments! You'll want the cans far enough apart so that you can hear the pitch of each can distinctly as it's hit.

With the Children:

1. While standing, hold the pitchmobile with one hand at each end and say something like, "This is my pitchmobile. Can you guess why I call it that?" Listen to responses and explain that it has different parts, like a glockenspiel, but it hangs in the air like a mobile.

2. Ask the children if they notice anything about the size of the cans. Children will observe that they're different sizes. Wonder aloud if the different sizes will make each can sound different when it's played. Listen to the children's ideas about this.

3. Ask the group how they think we could play it. They may say we could tap on the cans with our hands, or hit the cans with a mallet, or something else entirely. If an idea is possible, let them try it.

4. While one child is playing the pitchmobile, there should be two children, one on each end, facing inward, to hold it up. You can ask the children why it wouldn't be a good idea for one person to hold it while another person plays. They'll know it's because we don't want anyone to get hit with the cans, or accidentally hit with a mallet. When they've heard various ways to play the pitchmobile, let each child have a turn to play it.

Exploring the Science of Sounds: 100 Musical Activities for Young Children

5. Then ask the children if they think the cans would sound the same on the floor. Have a child try hitting the cans (carefully) while you hold each can on the floor. The sound won't be as loud, because your hands are stopping the vibration.

Questions to Ask

- How did the pitchmobile make sounds?
- What are the cans made out of? Can you think of other instruments made of metal?
- How does the metal make it sound? Would the pitchmobile sound different if we made it with plastic or paper cups?
- How did the different sizes affect the sounds of the cans?
- How did the structure of the mobile—with the cans hanging in the air—affect the sound?

Discoveries to Make

- Differently sized cans produce different pitches when hit.
- The cans sound louder when hit in the air than when they're held still on the floor.

Remember to emphasize the bigger concepts behind this activity—that size is related to pitch (a proportional relationship), that the cans don't make sound by themselves, but only when we hit them (cause and effect), and that hanging in the air lets the vibrations move through the air freely (structure affects function).

These concepts need to be spelled out to be reinforced. Also, recognizing the concepts in different contexts gives children a deeper understanding.

 GLASSES WITH DIFFERENT PITCHES

Here you'll be exploring how size and thickness affect the pitch of glasses. I wanted children to explore the unique sound of glass because it produces beautiful, clear tones. And glass is one of the relatively few materials that produces a pitch when tapped.

What You'll Need

5-6 glasses of various shapes, sizes, and thicknesses

Metal spoons and unsharpened pencils for tapping

Activity to Try

1. This should be done at a table, with a few children at a time, to ensure each child has time to investigate the sounds. Have the glasses set out in a row, each with a spoon or pencil. (Avoid extremely thin glassware that may be easily broken.) Remind the children not to touch the glasses until you ask them to.

2. Let one child at a time tap each glass, and ask them to think about the sounds, especially the higher and lower pitches. Caution them to be careful when tapping. (Actually, it's so rare that they're allowed to do something like this that they tend to take it very seriously, and tap with concentration and gentleness.)

Questions to Ask

- Did each of the glasses make the same sound?
- Can you think of reasons why they might have sounded different?
- Which glass had the lowest pitch? Which had the highest pitch?
- Why do you think some glasses had high pitches and some had low pitches?

Discoveries to Make

- Glasses of varying shapes, sizes, and heights have different pitches.
- Smaller glasses had higher pitches than bigger ones, confirming the principle that smaller-sized objects produce higher pitches.

Children often ask, "What's glass made of?" Most glass is made from a variety of materials, primarily silicon dioxide, or quartz. The materials are mixed together and melted in ovens that reach temperatures of nearly three thousand degrees! (For comparison, I say that on a really hot day in summer, the air temperature might be a hundred degrees.) Then the hot, melty glass is formed into windows, bottles, and other things. But how exactly does a mixture of silicon dioxide and other materials turn into glass? Good question. The Nobel physicist P. W. Anderson stated: *"The deepest and most interesting unsolved problem in solid state theory is probably the theory of the nature of glass and the glass transition."* (Anderson, 1995). One of your students may be the scientist to solve this problem one day!

THE PUPPIES AND
THE BIG DOGS

In "The Pitchmobile" and other activities, children confirmed the relationship between physical size and pitch, or how high or low a tone is. Now you'll demonstrate this knowledge in a game about two differently sized, and differently sounding, animals—puppies and big dogs. Children will also have the opportunity to demonstrate their awareness of the concept of pitch by taking turns playing high and low sounds on the glockenspiel.

What You'll Need

A glockenspiel

1-2 mallets

Activity to Try

1. Place the glockenspiel on the floor in front of you. Introduce the activity by asking the children if they remember which bars make the highest sounds and which make the lowest sounds. They should remember this, and you can confirm their answer by playing the highest notes (on the shortest bars) and the lowest notes (on the longest bars).

2. Ask the children to think about a puppy and a big dog. Which would they say has a higher-pitched voice and why? They should realize that a puppy is smaller than a big dog, and that's why it has a higher-pitched voice.

3. Explain the game. When you play high notes on the glockenspiel (demonstrate), the children should bark like puppies. Ask them to show you how a puppy barks. If you play the low notes (demonstrate), they should bark like big dogs. Ask them what that would sound like.

4. Whenever you stop playing, they should stop barking.

5. Explain that it might be hard to hear the glockenspiel when they're all barking. If they can't hear the glockenspiel, how will they know when you stop playing? Children should answer that they'll need to watch you. (It's a good idea, whenever you stop playing, to raise the mallets off the glockenspiel with a strong, sudden movement, so it's very obvious.)

6. Start the game! Remember to vary the duration of the "puppy" playing and the "big dog" playing, so the children really have to pay attention.

Questions to Ask

- A puppy is a very young dog, like a baby dog. Can you think of other baby animals that make higher-pitched sounds than their parents?
- What animals do you think make the highest sounds?
- Which animals make the lowest sounds?
- Do you think a baby animal will always make a higher-pitched sound than a grown-up animal? Why do you think so?

Discovery to Make

Children can respond to musical cues and visual cues to bark like a puppy, bark like a big dog, and stop barking.

> **KEEP THE LEARNING GOING!**
>
> Bring the glockenspiel and mallets with you when children have outdoor play.
>
> Some of them may enjoy continuing the "puppy and big dog" game with other animals. How about kittens and cats, chicks and chickens, or ducklings and ducks? Outside, they also have the space to act out the animal movements.

THE BIG ELEPHANT STOMP

The goal of this activity is to help children understand the relationship between low sounds and large size objects (or in this case, animals) in a fun, whole-body experience—to feel it in a way that engages many senses. Their ears hear the comically low, loping music; their arms, core, and legs are involved in the locomotor movement of the heavy, loud stomp; and their whole bodies can sense, through cooperating in a group movement, the feeling of being part of a very big animal. Best of all, from the young child's point of view, it's elephant-sized fun!

What You'll Need

A recording of "elephant music"

My suggestion:"V. The Elephant" from *The Carnival of the Animals* by Camille Saint-Saens. This is a slow, funny waltz.

There are lots of elephant songs, but this piece has the low, heavy, lumbering sound that's perfect for this activity.

Activity to Try

1. Tell the children that you're thinking of a very big animal. Ask them if they think this animal will make a high sound or a low sound. They should know it will make a low sound. You can give them hints, such as "This animal is gray . . . and lives in the jungle . . . and has big ears . . ." (You probably won't have to get to "and a long trunk" before they guess "elephant.")

2. Explain that they're going to pretend to be elephants. They're going to be really big elephants—so big it's going to take five people to make one elephant!

3. Ask the five children on your left to join you in the middle of the circle. Tell them you're going to be the first elephant. Ask one of them to be the front of the elephant and make a trunk with their arms. Ask two more children to be the front legs. They should stand behind the front of the elephant and put their hands on her shoulders, one child's hands on the "front's" left shoulder, the other's on her right. The last two children will be the back legs of the elephant. They should put their hands on the middle children's shoulders.

4. Ask the "elephant" group to show you how they'd walk like an elephant.

5. Tell the class that you brought in a wonderful piece of music about an elephant, and the "elephant" can stomp around the circle to the music. Challenge them to keep together and walk like one stomping elephant!

6. Start the music and let the "elephant" stomp around the circle a few times. Then pause the music, tell them what a great elephant they were, and let them go back to their spots in the circle.

7. Ask the next five children in the circle to be the next elephant. Continue until each child has a turn to be part of an elephant.

Questions to Ask

- The person who wrote this music wanted it to remind people of a big elephant. Do you think he did a good job? Did the music sound like an elephant?

- Was it hard to stay together while you stomped around? How did you stay together so well?

- Was the music low-pitched or high-pitched? How did that help it sound like an elephant?

- Did the music help you to walk like an elephant? How?

Discoveries to Make

- Low-pitched music makes it easier to walk very heavily and steadily, like an elephant.

- Children can cooperate in a group to pretend to be one animal walking.

Your class may be interested to know that elephants make low sounds, not only with their voices, but by stomping on the ground. The sound made by their stomping feet is too low for people to hear—but other elephants can hear it from miles away!

DO THE CRICKET HOP!

I love listening to crickets. To me, it's music, the sweet soundtrack to summer nights, countless tiny creatures weaving their songs together. When one of the characters in Shakespeare's *The Tempest* describes the enchanted island where he lives by saying, "Sometimes a thousand twangling instruments/Will hum about mine ears," I always imagine some kind of magical crickets!

But back to science . . . Crickets make a high-pitched sound (by scratching one wing against the other) because they're small—a perfect example of the concept of pitch.

Plus, they hop! Young children love the challenge of doing the "Cricket Hop." (Their hands and feet stand in for the six legs.)

What You'll Need

A recording of "cricket music"

Some suggestions: "Pizzicato" from the ballet *Sylvia*, by Léo Delibes (this is delicate music with a perfect hopping rhythm)

"Music Box Dancer" by Frank Mills

"Shenandoah Valley Breakdown" by Alan Munde (a very fast bluegrass piece—this may be a little too stimulating if you have a very active group)

Jingle bell bracelets (optional)

Masking tape

Activity to Try

1. Tell the group that you're thinking of a small animal. Ask them if they think it will make high or low sounds.

2. Give the children some hints to guess the animal, such as "This animal is an insect . . . it's green . . . it chirps . . ." They'll know it's a cricket.

3. Ask the children if they've heard crickets chirping, and what they sound like. Listen to each child who wants to demonstrate a cricket sound.

4. Tell them that there's something else crickets do that's really interesting—they hop! And not just on their back legs but on all six legs at the same time. Invite children to try hopping on their hands and feet. They should squat first, and then put their hands on the floor. Ask them to be careful of their neighbors, and try a hop. (You could also demonstrate the "Cricket Hop" yourself. I usually do, even though I feel like a particularly clumsy coffee table galumphing across the room. Luckily, my students are much more cricket-like!)

5. After they've tried it, have the children sit again.

152 *Exploring the Science of Sounds: 100 Musical Activities for Young Children*

6. Tell the children that they're each going to get a turn to do the "Cricket Hop" to music in this game. Bring out the masking tape, and make a line, about five to six feet long, inside the circle. Wonder aloud if you can hop all the way down the line. Hop down the line in three or four hops, to model that you're not trying to cover the whole space in one gigantic hop, as many adventurous children always want to do.

7. Start the music and have one child at a time do the "Cricket Hop." If you'd like, the nonhopping children can provide accompaniment with jingle bell bracelets (shaking them inside cupped hands makes a nice, quiet jingle) to sound like crickets chirping.

TIP

Children enjoy it when I call them up for their turn using their cricket names, like "Fiona Cricket" or "Parth Cricket."

Questions to Ask

- Do you think that was the right kind of music for pretending to be crickets hopping? Why? (Or why not, if someone says it wasn't.)
- Did the jingle bells sound like crickets chirping? What other instruments could we have used?
- If crickets were as big as dinosaurs, do you think they would sound the same? Why or why not?

Discoveries to Make

- High-pitched music and instruments can add fun to a game about small animals, by reminding us of the animals' sounds.
- Children can hop forward on their hands and feet like crickets.

 TUBULAR TONES

I wouldn't call myself an impulse shopper, but sometimes I can't resist buying an instrument, CD, or other item that I'm sure my students will absolutely love—except they don't. They sit with glazed-over eyes or suddenly remember an urgent need to show me their boo-boos or tattle on their friends. The poor whatever-it-was I'd been so excited about gets shoved to the back of my closet.

So although I'd been thinking about getting a set of tuned plastic percussion tubes for a while, I resisted the urge to splurge (I could see they'd take up a lot of space in the back of the closet) for years. Finally, of course, I gave in, and I'm so glad I did! They're colorful, they make a fabulous sound, and children really do love them. And they're made-to-order for exploring the size-pitch relationship with young children.

What You'll Need

Set of 8 tuned plastic percussion tubes (diatonic scale)

Activity to Try

1. Place the tubes in a closed box or bag next to you.

2. Tell the children that you brought in something really interesting. Bring out one of the tubes and ask if anyone knows what it is, or what it might be. Listen to their responses.

3. If no one is familiar with the tube, tell the class that it's a tuned plastic tube. Tell them "tuned" means that when you play it, it makes a musical tone.

4. Demonstrate holding the tube in one hand and hitting it against the palm of your other hand. You'll need to be rather forceful to get a good sound, but show that it's not necessary to hit it really hard. You can also show the children the best way to get a great sound—to make contact with your palm at a place a few inches from the end of the tube. There are many other ways to play these, but this is the best method to avoid denting and warping the tubes.

5. Tell the group that there are more tubes in the box, and they're going to get a chance to play them, but not yet. Explain that they're going to look at the tubes and talk about what they observe.

6. Bring out all the tubes (not in size order) and spread them randomly around on the floor inside the circle. Remind the children not to touch them yet.

7. They'll notice right away that the tubes are different colors. Ask them why they think the tubes are made in different colors. Listen to their ideas.

8. Children should also notice that the tubes are different sizes. Wonder aloud if the different sizes might have anything to do with how they sound. Do your students have any thoughts about this? They should remember that smaller things make higher sounds than larger things.

9. Observe aloud that each tube is a different size. Tell the children that they're going to arrange them in order by size, and when they're all in order, they can play them to hear if the tones get higher and higher as the tubes get smaller. Ask them which tube they think is the biggest.

10. Have a child come sit at the front of the room, facing the class. Hand her the biggest tube and have her hold it vertically on the floor. Then ask which tube is the biggest one left on the floor, and have that child sit next to the first with that tube. Continue until the children are sitting with the tubes in size order.

11. Now comes the fun part! Have the children with the tubes stand and spread out a bit. Have them play the tubes as you demonstrated, one at a time—biggest to smallest and then smallest to biggest.

12. Of course, every student will want a turn to play, and should have one, but I suggest having the discussion first, while the children's memory of the exploration is still fresh.

Questions to Ask

- What did you observe about the size of the tubes and the sounds they made?
- Do the tubes remind you of any other musical instrument we've played? (The graduated lengths and tones are similar to the structure of a glockenspiel.)
- Why did the tubes get higher as they got smaller?

Discovery to Make

Tuned plastic tubes demonstrate that smaller things make higher sounds than larger things.

> **TIP**
>
> Tuned plastic tubes are lots of fun but should be played only with adult supervision. They're very safe when played correctly, but young children can get overexcited and cause accidents. Also, the tubes can be damaged by overzealous playing.

CHAPTER SEVEN

OUTSIDE SOUNDS: THE SCIENCE OF NATURAL AND ENVIRONMENTAL SOUNDS

A Note to Teachers:

Have you ever watched the faces of young children as they leave the building and go outside to the playground? The joy and sheer relief are palpable. It's not that they don't have fun indoors—of course they do. It's just that grown-ups are so used to being cooped up inside, you don't even realize you're cooped up. But children do.

Dogs barking, birds singing, the leaves rustling and swishing in the wind—all the sounds of the great outdoors, which we relegate to the background of our attention, take center stage in the young child's sensory world.

KEY CONCEPT

Different animals, environmental phenomena, and natural objects make different sounds.

They may not always listen to grown-ups' directions, but they'll follow the sound of a buzzing fly indefinitely.

Every time I'm outside with young children, they have questions galore about the sounds they hear.

"Why is that plane so loud?"

"Why is the swing making that weird sound?"

"Why do birds sing so much?"

Don't let a "Why?" go by.

I try not to give an easy answer like "The plane is loud because it's so big." I caught myself saying that once and realized, "I don't even know if that's true. Actually I don't really know what I'm talking about!" The best answer to questions like these is "That's a great question—let's find out!" By building on the knowledge and understanding the children now have about the science of sounds, you'll be able to help them discover more about the sounds of the outside world.

It's great to have this discussion outside, if possible. Have the group get comfortable on the grass, or bring out a blanket if your playground area is all hard rubber and/or pavement. Talk about how we hear a lot of sounds outside that we don't hear inside. What are some of those sounds?

Keep this talk informal—we don't need to get into details yet. Make sure everyone gets a turn to talk about interesting outdoor sounds they've heard.

You may want to write down their thoughts for your own future reference. There may be running themes in their ideas—sounds they're especially interested in. Animal sounds, vehicles, "scary" sounds like barking dogs or thunder—different groups of children often have certain kinds of sounds they want to know more about.

When everyone's contributed to the discussion, compliment them on thinking of so many sounds. They're going to be learning more about all of them!

THE SOUNDS OF RAIN

Notice that this exploration is about the sounds of rain—plural. Rain can be anything from a light drip-drop to a torrential downpour. It can be a frightening sound, especially when it comes on suddenly . . . or a soothing one when you're going to sleep at night. Rain makes different sounds depending on where it lands, too—on the roof of a car, on treetops filled with leaves, on pavement, or on pools and puddles. Exploring these sounds gives children lots to think about—especially in the areas of loudness and timbre.

What You'll Need

A rainy day

Plastic pails, buckets, containers, and cups—one item for each child

Big (metal) soup pot

Activity to Try

1. It's a beautiful rainy day! Tell the class that you're going to go out in the rain and listen to its sounds. Have the children get into their rain gear and give each child a pail or other container.

2. When you're all outside, ask the children to let the rain fall into their pails. Ask them how it sounds—is it loud or soft? Ask if they can hear the individual raindrops hitting the bottom of the pail. Maybe they could make up words to describe the sounds they hear; you could get the ball rolling by describing the rain falling into your pail as sounding like "*dup dup dup*" or "*plink plink*." (Making up words for these rain sounds helps children to listen more closely.) Gather the children around the soup pot to listen to the rain falling on metal.

3. Have the children place their pails down on the ground. Suggest that everyone tilt their heads up to face the rain coming down. Ask them how the rain sounds when it hits their faces—does it

sound the same as the rain in the pail?

4. Have the children listen to how the rain sounds when it hits the slide, the swings, and other playground equipment.

5. Ask the children to look for a good puddle. They can try stepping in the puddle and jumping in it. They can also toss pebbles in it, and stir the puddle-water with sticks.

6. Before you go back inside, listen to the rain falling into the pails, which should have an inch or two of rain inside them. Ask the children what that sounds like.

Questions to Ask

- How did the rain sound when it fell on your face? What about when it fell in the empty pail?
- Which was louder, tossing pebbles in the puddle, or jumping in the puddle yourself? Why?
- Did the rain always sound exactly the same?
- Why didn't it always sound the same?

Discoveries to Make

- Rain has different timbres, depending on what kind of object or material it falls on.
- More forceful movements will produce louder sounds.

DON'T WORRY ABOUT BEING REPETITIVE

I sometimes think children will get bored or tune out if they keep hearing me talk about the relationship between force and loudness and similar principles. Well, maybe if I said the same things ten times a day, they would. But repetition is a powerful learning tool. I like this quote: "Anything I really need folks to remember and understand I need to repeat around fifteen times, on average, depending on how important the message is. The trick, or science, to doing this is not so much *saying* the same thing over and over again, but packaging it in different ways, and in different forms." The business consultant Terry St. Marie said this about working with adults. How much more would this advice apply to teaching young children?

A WALK FOR LISTENING AND UNDERSTANDING

The idea of a "listening walk" is nothing new, and calling children's attention to the variety of sounds outside is always valuable. It promotes their ability to focus, as well as their appreciation for the sounds of nature. After students have done some exploration in the science of sounds, a listening walk can be an even richer experience. This activity helps children apply their scientific reasoning to understand the sounds they hear, to hear familiar sounds in new ways, and to become even more curious about the world around them.

What You'll Need

A notebook and a pen or pencil, for yourself

Activity to Try

1. Before you take the group outside, explain that you're all going on a special "listening walk." Explain that you want them to listen very carefully to all of the sounds outside. They may hear sounds that are very familiar and can also try to find sounds they haven't listened to before. When they notice a sound, they can tell you, and you'll write it down so you can all talk about it later. But they should remember that you can hear only one person at a time, so just as in the classroom, if they raise their hand it will help you to listen to every student. They may need reminding that more than one of them might hear the same sound. In fact, it's very likely. (This may head off arguments of who heard the garbage truck first.)

2. When you're outside, model quiet, attentive listening—don't speak if it's not necessary. Walking around the playground is fine; you don't need to go far to hear a lot of sounds! Jot down the sounds the children tell you about. To respond, try to just raise your eyebrows and nod in appreciation, rather than speaking.

3. Back in the classroom, engage the children in a discussion about the sounds they heard.

Questions to Ask

- When children mention a sound they heard, you could ask:
- Where did the sound come from?
- Was it soft or loud?
- Why do you think it sounded soft (or loud)?
- How far away do you think the sound was? Why?
- Did the sound have a pitch, like (sing a few notes, "*la la la*"), or was it an unpitched sound like a motor or a knock on a door?
- Was the sound's timbre sharp, like metal, or flat, like plastic, or was the timbre more like a voice?
- Did the sound have a beat, like a song or a bouncing ball?
- Tell the group that when they discuss different parts of something, like we talked about the loudness, timbre, and pitch of each sound, that's called analyzing. Tell them they analyzed the sounds they heard.
- Were the sounds we heard mostly the same, or did we hear lots of different sounds?

Discoveries to Make

- The world is filled with many different kinds of sounds.
- Children can analyze sounds by talking about their various parts, such as loudness, tempo, pitch, and timbre.

KEEP THE LEARNING GOING!

Try to call the children's attention to listening, in various ways, throughout the day. Mention sounds you hear; for instance, you can say, "I hear something ringing, do you hear it? What is it?" when the phone rings. During free play it's fun to play a game where you close your eyes and have a student make a sound with a toy or other object. You can try to guess what the sound is. Then trade places.

 WIND CHIMES

There's something special and dreamlike about the sound of wind chimes. Whatever they're made of, whether they clink, clatter, or ring, the constantly changing wind patterns make them seem to move on their own, sometimes strong and resonant, sometimes delicate and whispering.

Young children are enchanted by wind chimes and very curious about their sounds. In this activity, you'll explore wind chimes of varying timbres and sizes.

What You'll Need

A windy day

Many different wind chimes of metal, plastic, and other timbres

Mallets or unsharpened pencils

Activity to Try

1. While still inside, tell the children that they'll be listening to wind chimes and analyzing their sounds.
2. Bring the wind chimes out with you and have the children help you decide where to hang them. Ideally, they should hang freely on a tree branch or porch railing. You can use fences or gates, or other places where they won't be completely free to move in the wind, as long as they'll make some sound.
3. Let the children wander from one set of wind chimes to another, but ask them to be fairly quiet so we can all listen carefully. Ask them not to touch the wind chimes, since that would change the sound. If the wind dies down, they can use the mallets or unsharpened pencils to "strum" the chimes gently from one side to the other to mimic the wind's light movement.
4. After ten or fifteen minutes, gather the wind chimes and return to the classroom.

Questions to Ask

- Did you notice the wind chimes had different timbres? What timbres did you hear?
- Did you hear any difference in sound between the short, medium-sized, and long wind chimes?
- What if we shook the items that were hanging from the wind chimes in a big shaker, instead of a wind chime? Do you think the sound would be different or the same? Why?
- How did the wind chimes make sounds?

Discoveries to Make

- Wind can cause wind chimes to move, making the objects knock against each other and produce sounds.
- Children can analyze the wind chimes' sounds in terms of timbre and loudness.

SINGING BIRDS

I used to think birds were the only animals, aside from humans, that could sing. Was I ever wrong! Even if you don't count insects or whales, both of whom make nonvocal "singing" sounds, there are still plenty of examples of singers in the animal kingdom. Bats, in particular, use very sophisticated vocal singing to communicate. Researchers at Texas A & M University found that "No other mammals besides humans are able to use such complex vocal sequences to communicate" (Texas A & M University, 2007). The singing of birds, though, is very familiar to young children and very intriguing too.

There are two kinds of bird singing—songs and calls. Songs are used for courtship and mating, while calls are used more for alarms and keeping a flock together. Both songs and calls are very complex. Young birds actually learn how to sing from their fathers and other adults—it isn't instinctive behavior. Birds are among the most intelligent animals.

Young children are usually very interested in birds and their songs. As teachers we can, and should, encourage this interest in birds, especially birds that are part of our local ecosystems.

What You'll Need

To prepare for this activity, it helps to have some kind of guide to bird songs and calls. The Cornell Lab of Ornithology has a remarkably comprehensive website, "All About Birds," at https://www.allaboutbirds.org/guide/search. It includes information on how to identify each species, videos, and audio of songs and calls. Many websites can tell you the birds in your state or region.

The company Wild Republic makes Audubon plush birds in a variety of species. The birds were created in conjunction with the Audubon Society and feature recordings of songs from the Cornell Lab. (They sing when gently squeezed.) They're adorable and most are under ten dollars. They're certainly not necessary for this activity, but they're nice to have to help children remember "their bird."

Activity to Try

Ahead of Time:

Decide on a bird to focus on in this activity. It's a special experience for young children to learn to recognize the appearance and song of one bird. Hopefully they'll be excited to learn about more birds, but there's plenty to learn about and experience with just one. Make sure you know when the bird you've chosen will be in your area, if it's not year-round. (If you know of a certain species with a nest near your facility, so much the better!)

I've always loved robins, and they're found all over North America. They're easy to recognize and sing a charming song. In the winter, I talk with the children about Canada geese. Their honking call is very distinctive, as is their "V" formation flying pattern.

With the Children:

1. Talk to the class about the bird you'll be watching and listening for. (I'll use a robin in this example). Show them a photo of the bird. You can point out its features, especially its rounded shape and orange-red front. Explain that each kind of bird has its own special song, and that when we see a robin outside, you'll hear it singing its robin song.

2. If you have one of the Audubon plush birds, show it to the children, but let them discover the song for themselves, outside, from real birds, before you share the toy's song with them.

3. Take the children outside and have a "robin hunt." It shouldn't take long before a robin is spotted. Do they hear the bird's song? Ask the children to listen quietly.

4. It's very exciting for them to "find" a robin and hear it sing. Ask them if they can copy the song. Robins sing in a much higher pitch than we do, but the rhythm is easy to copy. (Supposedly it sounds like *cheer up, cheer up, cheer up.*")

5. It may not be scientific, but when children want to talk to the robin in its "language," I don't discourage them. I've found that when they do this, they usually feel a bond with the bird, which is wonderful.

6. Return to the classroom after ten or fifteen minutes.

Questions to Ask

- Who remembers the robin's song?
- (Listen to every child who wants to sing it for you.)
- Did the robin sing in a high or low pitch?
- Without a photo or toy visible, ask, "Do you remember what the robin looked like?"
- Why do you think the robin sang in a high pitch?
- Do you think a bigger bird, like a turkey, would have a lower-pitched song?
- (If they're not sure, you can go online with them and find out!)

Discoveries to Make

- Each kind of bird has its own song.
- The relationship between size and pitch applies to birds as well as objects.

KEEP THE LEARNING GOING!

Now your students have learned the basics about robins—but don't let it end there! Think of it this way—the children have met some new neighbors. Now those neighbors can be friends. See if the class can find the robins whenever there's outdoor playtime. Make it a game for them to guess whether they'll hear or see the robins first.

They may want to make a bird feeder for them. This activity may also inspire children to want to learn about more of the birds in their neighborhood. Let their interest be your guide in continuing your bird explorations.

 BUZZING BEES

For many children, the sound of a buzzing bee means only one thing—a sting might be coming! It's good to be careful, but buzzing is also a sign that an interesting and important insect is hard at work. In this activity, children listen to bees, learn about what the bees are doing, and enjoy some buzzing and flying of their own.

What You'll Need

A bee, if you happen to hear one outside

Masking tape

A recording of "bee music"—I suggest "Flight of the Bumblebee" by Rimsky-Korsakov. This old standby really does sound like a buzzing bee, in its sound and in its urgent, racing tempo. There are many versions available, but I like the solo violin version—it's by far the buzziest.

Activity to Try

This activity will be most effective if you wait until the first time in spring when children hear a bee. That first buzz is exciting and sparks some fears, but curiosity, too. I've heard questions like, "Why don't they just fly away and leave us alone?" and "How do they buzz like that?" What a great opportunity to learn about bees!

1. Begin by asking if anyone knows what bees eat. Some children will say "honey," because they associate honey with bees. Some will know that bees eat nectar from flowers. Some will know that they also eat pollen. If the children don't know what these substances are, explain that pollen is that yellow, powdery stuff you see on flowers sometimes, and nectar is a liquid, like juice. Both are actually made by the flowers.

2. Ask the children how they think that baby bees, who can't fly yet, get their food. Children will realize that the grown-up bees have to bring food to the baby bees. The grown-up bees, called worker bees, have to keep going out of the hive to get pollen and nectar for the babies, who are called larvae. It's a lot of work because larvae eat more than a thousand meals a day!

3. Ask the children if they can buzz like bees, and listen to the room fill with their energetic buzzing!

4. Point out that we buzzed with our mouths. Ask the children how they think that bees buzz. Some may guess that their wings, moving very fast, create the buzzing sound. Tell them that's true—bees have to move their wings very fast to fly. That's the vibration that creates the buzzing sound. Tell the class that they're going to play a game where they pretend to be worker bees getting pollen and nectar to feed the larvae.

5. Get out masking tape and make a line down the middle of the circle. Explain that one side of the room will be the hive, and the other side will be the outside, where the flowers are.

6. Ask if anyone would like to pretend to be the larvae—the baby bees. Sometimes there will be eager volunteers for this role, but if not, you can use stuffed animals to be the larvae. All the larvae and worker bees should come over to the hive. The worker bees should be standing. Explain that when you start the music, worker bees should fly out of the hive, moving their "wings" (arms with bent elbows) quickly, and buzzing, to get pollen and nectar for the larvae. Remind them to be careful not to bump into any of the other bees. They should gather a lot of food, because those larvae are always hungry! When the music stops, that's their signal to come back to the hive and feed the larvae. When the music starts again, it's time to fly out for more food!

7. Start playing "Flight of the Bumblebee." Worker bees should fly out, buzzing, and pretend to get food. After a while, pause the music. Worker bees should return to the hive and feed the larvae. Go through this cycle three or four times.

8. After the game, have the children return to their seats.

Questions to Ask

- Why do the worker bees have to fly around so fast? What are they doing?
- Do you remember what kind of food bees eat?
- How do bees buzz?

Discoveries to Make

- Bees buzz by moving their wings very fast when they fly.
- Worker bees have to fly very fast to gather food—pollen and nectar from flowers—to feed the larvae, or baby bees, back in the hive.

Bees pollinate a third of everything we eat and play a vital role in sustaining the planet's ecosystems. Today many bee species are endangered. You can explore the website Mother Nature Network at http://www.mnn.com/family/family-activities/stories/5-ways-to-help-children-help-bees, to learn ways that the children can help to protect bees.

"THE OAK TREE SONG"

Acorns are one of my favorite natural musical instruments. You can tap them together or shake them in pails for a clear, clicky, solid sound. You can even make music with their cute little caps, stringing them together and shaking them in softly rustling bracelets and necklaces.

For this activity, though, you're going to stick to shaking the whole acorn. And you'll use them to illustrate how the wind blows acorns from the oak tree—one of fall's prettiest natural sounds.

What You'll Need

An oak tree in the fall, with plenty of fallen acorns

One acorn for your introductory talk

Containers, one for each child

Activity to Try

1. Show the group an acorn and ask the children if they've seen acorns outside. Ask them if they know what acorns are. Some may know that acorns are nuts that come from oak trees, containing seeds that can grow to become more oak trees. Ask if anyone has heard or seen the wind blowing acorns to the ground.
2. Tell them that you're going to play a singing game using acorns. Give each child a plastic pail or other small container. Tell them you're going outside to collect a handful or so of acorns each and put them in the containers. Remind them not to throw the acorns.
3. Go outside and allow several minutes for gathering acorns.
4. When everyone has enough acorns in their container, form a standing circle, on a hard surface. Tell the children that they're all going to pretend to be oak trees. They're going to sing a song about the wind blowing the acorns off the trees.
5. Ask the children how they would stand if they were oak trees. If they're not sure, encourage them to observe the oak tree. Is it tall? Straight?
6. When you're all standing like oak trees (but still holding the containers), sing to the tune of "Six Little Ducks":

> *There was an oak tree standing tall,*
> *Leaves turning colors in the fall,*
> *One day a soft little breeze came around,*
> *And one little acorn fell to the ground.*

7. Everyone should take one acorn from their container and drop it to the ground.

8. Repeat twice, each time with "one more acorn" falling to the ground.

9. Then sing:

> *There was an oak tree standing tall,*
> *Leaves turning colors in the fall,*
> *One day a great big wind came around,*
> *And all of the acorns fell to the ground!*

10. Then the children can drop all the acorns to the ground! Whee! They love this and will want to do it again immediately! Remind them to walk carefully around the acorns.

11. Return inside and go back to the circle.

Questions to Ask

- What did we learn about acorns? What are they? Where do they come from?
- If an acorn grows in the ground, what will it become?
- When one acorn fell on the hard surface, what did it sound like? Did it sound hard like a pebble, or soft like a marshmallow?
- How do you think it would sound if we dropped it on the grass?
- If they're not sure, go out and try it.
- What about when all the acorns fell? Was the sound different?

<table>
<tr><td>TIP</td></tr>
<tr><td>Throughout the school year, children can observe the life cycle of the oak trees. They can note the leaves gradually falling off the tree, the fresh leaves sprouting in the spring, and the way the new leaves grow and deepen in color.</td></tr>
</table>

Discoveries to Make

- Acorns have a hard sound when dropped on a hard surface.
- Many acorns falling make more noise than one acorn, since the force of many acorns adds up to one large force, creating a louder sound.
- Acorns are nuts containing seeds that can grow to be oak trees.
- Children learned the pattern, or cycle, of oak trees producing acorns, which can grow to be oak trees.

WHAT THE BIRDS HEARD

With this activity, you're revisiting the proportional relationship between distance and loudness. Sounds get louder as they move closer and softer as they move farther away. Instead of moving the sources of sound, as we did in "Shakers Near and Far" and other activities, here you're considering the perspective of listeners who are closer or farther away from a nonmoving source of sound. We also have some fun pretending to be birds!

What You'll Need

No materials needed

Activity to Try

1. The class should be sitting in a circle outside. Tell them you're going to play a game about how things sound, depending on whether you're close or far away from the sound. Ask them if they remember the game played with the paper birds that flew closer and closer in the "Paper Birds" activity. Listen to the children's responses. Ask them if the birds sounded louder when they were far away, or when they got close. Children will remember that the birds sounded louder as they flew closer.

2. Tell them that they're going to think about real birds and how they might hear things from way up in the sky. Take a minute to have the children point out the birds they see in the sky.

3. Ask the children if a car driving by sounds loud or soft. Ask if anyone can make a sound like a car, and listen to the children's sounds. Then ask them if they were way up in the sky, like a bird, if the car would sound the same from up there. They'll know that it would sound much softer. Ask them how they think it would sound from way up there. Again, listen to the children's sounds.

4. Have children form two groups. (It's easiest to just split the circle down the middle.) Have one group be people on the ground, and tell the other group to pretend they're birds in the sky. They may tweet and flap their wings a bit if they wish.

5. Tell the children you're imagining you hear a dog barking. Ask the "people" group what the dog sounds like. The "people" group will bark loudly. Then turn to the "birds" and ask them what the dog sounds like from up in the sky. The "birds" should bark very softly.

6. Continue the game, imagining sounds like a baby crying, children running, a bouncing ball, and so on. Let the children suggest ideas for sounds. They may want to hear sounds not usually associated with the playground, such as a cow, a pig, a lion, or a dinosaur. Remember to switch the sides after a while so both groups can enjoy being the birds. And of course, "imagine" each sound in a playful, casual way–this is a game, not a test!

Questions to Ask

- When we hear a loud sound, like a barking dog, does it sound the same to birds in the sky?
- What about if we heard a soft sound, like a kitten meowing? Do you think the bird would hear it?
- Why do sounds on the ground sound softer to the birds?

Discoveries to Make

- Children discovered the proportional relationship between distance and sound in a new context.
- Children considered distance in a vertical sense, rather than horizontal.

KEEP THE LEARNING GOING!

You can "turn the game around" by imagining sounds that originate in the sky, such as thunder, airplanes, or geese honking. How would the birds and people hear those sounds?

THE OUTSIDE ORCHESTRA

The students have explored many outside sounds, including rain, acorns, buzzing bees, and more. But there are so many sounds to be found outdoors! The sonic ecosystem is rich in objects and materials to be tapped, scratched, shaken, rubbed, blown on, strummed, knocked on, stirred, patted, jumped on . . . the possibilities are endless. This activity provides an opportunity for children to investigate further and get creative.

What You'll Need

Some mallets and brushes

Pails and plastic containers, with and without lids

Metal and plastic spoons

Anything else you can use to (harmlessly) tap outdoor objects

Activity to Try

1. Gather your materials in a box or basket and take them out to the playground. Children should be sitting in a circle while you explain the activity. Remind them that they've heard some interesting sounds outside. Ask them which sounds they remember. Listen to their responses.

Exploring the Science of Sounds: 100 Musical Activities for Young Children

2. Ask them whether they've ever wondered about other ways we could make music and sounds with things they see outside. Again, listen to their ideas. If there are some you haven't thought of (and there will be!), think about how you could help the children make them happen.

3. Tell the children that you thought it would be fun to investigate other ways we can make sounds outside. One by one, show them the items you've brought. Tell the group that they may use these to explore sounds outside by gently tapping or shaking things. They can also use their hands—to tap things together, to shake things in the air, to roll things on the ground, stir things around, and so on. They are free to use the playground equipment, trees, the pavement or hard rubber surface of the playground, gates and fences, small pebbles, acorns, dry leaves, sticks and twigs, pinecones on the ground, balls, and other outdoor toys. Remind them that grass, and leaves still on the trees, are alive and growing–these should be off limits. If they're not sure whether something is okay to use, they should ask you first.

4. Tell them that after a while you'll call them back to the circle, and they can share how they made music and sounds.

5. While the children are exploring, stay fairly close, listen, and enjoy. If someone's having trouble creating a certain sound, be supportive ("I like the way you're trying different solutions," "That's an interesting idea," "Maybe there's another way") but avoid stepping in to "help."

6. When it looks as if each child has had some sound-making adventures, regroup and have the children share their experiences. They can also recreate the sounds for the group (for instance, shaking objects in a container).

Questions to Ask

- Was there anything that surprised you when you explored making sounds?
- Can you think of anything else we could bring outside to help us make music and sounds with the materials and objects out here?
- Is there anything you didn't get a chance to do, that you'd like to try next time you're outside?
- (If children volunteer ideas, write them down and make sure they get a chance to try out these ideas soon.)
- Do you think we need musical instruments, CD players, and phones to make music, or can we use things we find outside?

Discovery to Make

Children can make a wide variety of music and sounds with materials and objects they find outdoors.

USING OUTSIDE SOUNDS TO ACCOMPANY A STORY

Putting learning into an actively creative context is a great way for young children to make that learning their own. In this fun activity, students can put their understanding of the timbre and loudness of outside sounds to use by dramatically expressing a story in sound. As a bonus, it encourages problem-solving and cooperation.

What You'll Need

A read-aloud picture book featuring many outside sounds

Some suggestions: *Tick-Tock, Drip-Drop* by Nicola Moon

Tweedle Dee Dee by Charlotte Voake

Huff & Puff by Claudia Rueda

Railroad Hank by Lisa Moser

We're Going on a Leaf Hunt by Steve Metzger

Pails and bags to gather materials from outside

Activity to Try

1. This is a two-day activity. On the first day, read the story to your class. Ask the children to think about sounds they could make, using materials and objects from outside, to help tell the story when you read it again tomorrow. Explain that they might use sticks, leaves, small stones, acorns, pinecones, or other objects to represent sounds like branches, eggs cracking, bricks, and trees. They could also think of ways to represent wind, rain, creaking gates, and other sounds using objects from inside, or their own bodies (including their voices).

2. On the second day, review the story page by page and ask the children for ideas for sounds that go with the action on the page. Allow plenty of time for discussion. Some sounds may take more than one person to produce. Some sounds might require multiple objects—for example, a nest could be represented by dry leaves, pinecones, and twigs. Let the children go through a certain amount of trial and error to come up with the sounds they want. When you're finished collecting ideas, help the children plan when they'll make their sounds.

3. Tell them their cues—for example, when you read the word "gate," they'd make their creaking gate sound.

4. Read the story, with the children contributing their outside sounds.

Questions to Ask

- What did you think was different about reading the story with all the sounds in it? Was it more exciting? More realistic?
- Which part of the story was the hardest to think of a sound for?
- How did you decide which sound would go best with each part of the story?

Discoveries to Make

- Children can use their knowledge of outside sounds, as well as other sounds, to help tell a story and make it more interesting and expressive.
- Children can cooperate with others to come up with interesting ideas.

TIP

The sounds children decide on to accompany characters or actions in the story may seem unconventional or just plain weird. Once, I taught a boy who waved two sticks, held from his nose like a snout, to be the "sound" of a hedgehog. This didn't even make a sound, but all the children agreed it was a good choice. He used it in the story and everyone enjoyed it. It's more important to let children own this experience than to have a realistic, "correct" sound.

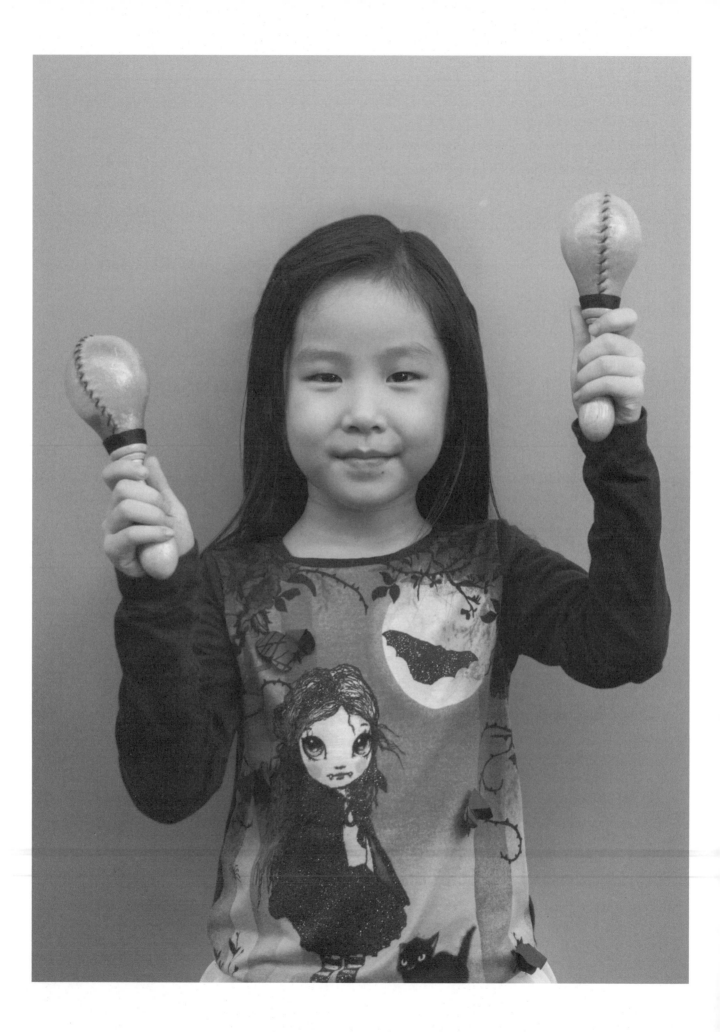

CHAPTER EIGHT

CREATING MUSICAL INSTRUMENTS

You'll need several metal, plastic, paper, and wooden objects and instruments, including large and small examples.

Tell the children they're going to be making their own musical instruments! There will be four projects: shakers, stringed instruments, drums, and wind chimes.

Discuss different materials, such as metal, plastic, rubber bands, and wood, and their timbres. Review the objects and instruments. Talk about how we can make loud and soft sounds with instruments. Ask the children how they would make an instrument have a high pitch—would they make it small or large?

KEY CONCEPT

We can use our knowledge of science and our creativity to make musical instruments.

This is a great time to remind the class that their instruments don't have to look perfect. It helps to have a few of your handmade instruments around, such as those from the "Tap Gloves" and "The Pitchmobile" activities. Unless you're an expert craftsperson, these instruments probably won't look like you bought them in a store. Instruments are for making music, not for looking fancy or beautiful. Tell the children they're going to make instruments, make music, and have fun!

CREATING SHAKERS WITH DIFFERENT TIMBRES

Children love shakers, and they have a lot of fun making shakers of their own. I've found that shakers made from clear plastic jars with screw-on lids are sturdier than those made from folded, stapled paper plates. They're more durable and less likely to leak.

What You'll Need

Clean plastic jars with lids, like peanut butter jars or honey jars

Newspaper or plastic to cover the worktable

Fillings, which may include bits of twigs, acorns, small pinecones, buttons, colored plastic or wooden beads, plastic tags, pebbles, small seashells, pennies, and plastic bottle caps

Glitter or stickers for decorating (optional)

Activity to Try

1. Have a few children at a time working at the table, which should be covered for easier cleanup. Before they start, talk with the children about what kind of timbre they want their shakers to have—hard and loud, soft and soothing, bumpy or smooth? Then ask them to think about which of the materials would produce that kind of timbre. Of course, they're free to use more than one filling, but they should think about how that will affect the sound.

2. If they're not happy with their sound when they're done, give them a chance to revise their thoughts on what materials they should use. They may find, for example, that the beans aren't as loud as they thought they would be—they might like to try macaroni instead. Children can learn a lot from trying, revising their designs and trying again.

Questions to Ask

- Throughout the activity, you should be available to supervise and ask questions as problems arise, such as "Hmm, do you think filling it so full will give the rice enough room to shake?" and "We're out of bottle caps—what else do you see that would make a hard, bumpy sound?"
- When all the projects are completed, have the children bring them to the circle to show to their classmates. Ask each child how she chose the materials to get the timbre she wanted.

Discoveries to Make

- Children can use their knowledge of the timbre of various materials to create a shaker with a distinctive timbre of its own.
- Creating instruments can involve trying things that don't work out, revising their plans, and trying again.

 CREATING STRINGED INSTRUMENTS

It's remarkably easy to build a basic stringed instrument that actually sounds pretty good. The challenge (and the fun) for young children is in tinkering with the structure and the rubber-band "strings" to get different pitches.

What You'll Need

Newspaper or plastic to cover the worktable

Shoe boxes or other sturdy boxes and lids

Lots of rubber bands (a mix of thin and thick, and small and large)

Duct tape or packing tape

Construction paper

Glue

Scissors

Crayons and markers for decoration (optional)

Activity to Try

1. Cover your worktable and have materials ready. A few children at a time can be working, so you can be available to encourage each child.

2. Each child can choose a container to be the base of the instrument. They can cover the container with construction paper and decorate it with crayons or markers, if they wish. They can decide if they want one whole side of the box open, or if they'd like a six-sided, closed box with a sound hole cut in one of the sides (they may need help with this).

3. Before the children wrap rubber bands around the box for the "strings," ask them what kind of sounds they'd like, higher-pitched sounds or lower-pitched sounds, or both. Ask them which kind of rubber bands they should use to get the pitches they want.

4. Children can wrap rubber bands around the box and try out their instrument by strumming and plucking the rubber bands.

5. Attaching the rubber bands to the sides of the box with duct tape or packing tape will help keep the pitches stable. Children can always remove the tape later to adjust the pitches.

> **TIP**
>
> Keep the children's homemade stringed instruments in the classroom for a week or two, to promote further exploration. Children love to strum their instruments while singing favorite songs or improvising their own. They'll want to share their songs with you and their friends, which gets even more students interested in playing and singing.

Questions to Ask

- What do the strings sound like when you pluck them? Do they sound better when you pluck hard or gently?

- (Encourage the children to experiment with this—they'll want to pluck hard enough for the sound to be heard but gently enough to produce a clear tone. Many children find it easier to pluck a string by using their thumb and forefinger to pinch it, rather than using the forefinger alone, as most adults do.)

- What would happen if you pulled the rubber bands tighter or made them looser? (Again, this is something they might want to experiment with.)

- What would happen if you pressed down on the string over the open side (or sound hole) with one finger and then plucked it with another?

- What are some ways we can change the pitch of a string on a stringed instrument?

Discoveries to Make

- Children can create their own stringed instruments.

- Children can change the pitch of each string by stretching it tighter (making the part of the string that is plucked smaller) or making it looser (which makes the plucked string larger).

- Children can also change the pitch of a string by pressing down on it over the open side or sound hole (effectively making a smaller string).

Exploring the Science of Sounds: 100 Musical Activities for Young Children

CREATING DRUMS THAT ARE MORE THAN DRUMS

Drums are almost too easy to make. Basically find a thing, bang on it, and boom, it's a drum. So rather than have this project be "decorating a can," I wanted to give students more to do and more to think about. How could we produce more sounds with drums? How many more sounds? And how would we play these new instruments?

This activity is more than a craft; it's an adventure in exploration and engineering. And children always come up with more ideas than I could have imagined.

What You'll Need

Coffee cans—one for each child

Newspaper or plastic to cover the worktable

Construction paper, crayons, and markers

4.5" x 5.5" sheets of sandpaper (I found packs of these at a dollar store)

Unsharpened pencils for mallets

Scissors and glue or double-sided tape

Small items for inside the drums, to shake—for instance, plastic bottle caps, building bricks, small bouncy balls, and buttons

Recording of music with a steady beat (See "Suggested Recordings of Instrumental Music on page 190")

Activity to Try

1. Tell the group that you're going to be making drums with coffee cans, but not just any drums. You'll be able to make lots of different sounds with these drums!

2. Have a few children at a time working at the table, which should be covered for easy cleanup.

3. Have all the materials out on the table. Children will probably ask why the sandpaper is there. Tell them that they can cut out sandpaper shapes to put on the side of the drum, and then scrape the sandpaper with the side of the pencil for a fun sound. They'll want to do that right away, so ask them if they want to cover the drum with construction paper and color on it first.

4. Children will need to decide the shapes they want, how much of the can to cover with sandpaper, and whether they want big shapes or little shapes. They can cut sandpaper in squares, triangles, or any kind of shape—or a jagged, irregular shape. They could cut the shape of a number or their initial (they might want your help). Remind the children that they'll need to leave enough of the can unsandpapered to be able to hold it comfortably while playing.

5. Children can glue the pieces of sandpaper on the can or stick them on with double-sided tape.

6. Let the children scrape the sandpaper with the side of the pencil. It's not a very exciting sound, and they'll tell you that. They'll wonder how to make a louder, "scrapier" scrape. Ask them to think about sand blocks—what makes the scraping sound? They'll realize the pencil needs to have sandpaper on it, too.

7. Children can cut a small strip, about one inch wide, to attach around the pencil. Ask them where on the pencil they should attach the sandpaper strip. They should think about how they'll scrape the side of the drum where the sandpaper is—what part of the pencil will be in contact with the sandpaper?

8. After they attach the sandpaper to the pencil, children can make this "scrapey" drum into a shaker, too! They can choose items to put inside. They'll get the most clatter if the drum is about one-third full of items. Ask them what kind of timbre they want—heavy, light, clicky, loud? Let them experiment a bit to find a timbre they like.

9. Make an instrument for yourself, too, so you can join the children when they play the instruments together.

10. When everyone's done, have them come back to the circle. Put on some background music.

11. Ask each child to demonstrate a sound he can make with his drum. They can use the pencil or their hands, and the top, bottom, and side of the can, to make any sounds they want. It's fun to play as a group too!

Questions to Ask

- Can you describe some of the timbres of this instrument?
- What were some of the ways we were able to play this instrument?
- How did you get the different timbres when you made your instrument?

Discoveries to Make

- Children can make a musical instrument with several different timbres.
- Different objects and materials can give musical instruments different timbres.

TIP

Play each rhythm pattern several times. Then invite the children to improvise their own patterns for the group to copy. These rhythms reinforce the concept of patterns in a fun, musical way.

TIP

This unique instrument lends itself to improvising rhythm patterns.

With some music in the background, take your drum and pencil and have children copy a few patterns, like:

"Tap tap shake shake scra-a-a-pe" (to the rhythm of "E-I-E-I-O") or

"Tap-py scrape-y shake shake" (to the rhythm of "it-sy bit-sy spi-der")

Play each rhythm pattern several times. Then invite the children to improvise their own patterns for the group to copy. These rhythms reinforce the concept of patterns in a fun, musical way.

CREATING WIND CHIMES WITH DIFFERENT TIMBRES

This is a very simple version of wind chimes. I wanted something that young children could create by themselves with a minimum of adult "help." You'll set up the frames beforehand, but students can decide the timbres they want, and how they'll arrange the items.

What You'll Need

Large plastic cups, one for each child and one for you

One pair of scissors (grown-up ones)

String

Hole punch

Duct tape or packing tape

Items to attach to the wind chimes' strings

Unsharpened pencils, one for each child

Newspaper or plastic to cover your worktable

Activity to Try

Ahead of Time:

Assemble the frames for the wind chimes. For each, punch four holes around the rim of a large plastic cup. Make a hole in the bottom with the scissors (this will be the top of the wind chime).

Cut five lengths of string about 12 inches long. Make big knots at the ends. Thread the strings through the holes so the knots secure them in place—one string to hang the wind chime from the top, and four to hang items from the bottom.

With the Children:

1. Cover the workspace and have a few children working at a time. Have a selection of items in the center. (Items may include plastic spoons, key chains with or without old keys, big and small plastic bottle caps, old CDs, seashells, old, unusable pens, old playing cards (they can click together in the wind), puzzle pieces that lost their puzzle, large wooden beads, and pennies.)

2. Give each child a frame. Explain that they can use one type of item or several, but they should think first about what they want their wind chime to sound like—what timbres they want.

3. Children may tape only a few items to each string or fill it from top to bottom, depending on whether they want a simple and spare sound or a more complex sound. You may need to cut smaller pieces of tape to help children attach smaller objects like seashells and pennies. Be sure everything is securely attached and there are no sharp edges.

4. When everyone's ready, gather the children in a circle. They can show their creations to the group and gently strum them with their fingers to demonstrate the timbre(s). They may also play the chimes by holding the top string and gently bouncing the chimes in the air.

> **TIP**
>
> When the activities using homemade instruments are over, weather permitting, create an outdoor gallery of the students' wind chimes for everyone to enjoy.

Questions to Ask

- How did you make your wind chime?
- How could you make it sound louder? Softer?
- Ask each child to describe the timbres of their wind chime and the items that give the instrument those timbres.

Discoveries to Make

- Children can create unique wind chimes by choosing and arranging items with different timbres.
- Children can describe the timbre(s) of their wind chimes to others.

 USING HANDMADE INSTRUMENTS TO ACCOMPANY SONGS

Making music together with their handmade instruments adds meaning and richness to the creative experience. Each one-of-a-kind instrument contributes its own special timbre(s) to the sound of the classroom band.

What You'll Need

Have each child choose her favorite of the instruments she created.

Activity to Try

1. Invite the children to suggest ideas for songs to sing and accompany with their instruments.

2. Encourage musical expressiveness. For example, ask if "Twinkle, Twinkle, Little Star" would sound better with a loud, boisterous accompaniment or a soft, delicate one.

3. To add more musicality, you could have the children accent certain beats by playing sharply on the "moo moo" and other animal sounds in "Old MacDonald."

4. You could also play a version of "If You're Happy and You Know It," highlighting different timbres: for instance, "If you have strings and you know it, strum your strings (strum strum)."

5. Children may also suggest ideas for playing songs with expressive changes in tempo or loudness, or with rhythmic accents.

> **TIP**
>
> Record this performance, if you can. It can help reinforce all the learning children put into this project to play the recording in a few weeks, or even months. Children like to remember and talk about their instruments, and about how they made them.

Questions to Ask

- Would anyone like to tell the class why you chose your instrument as your favorite? What did you especially like about it?

- Did it feel different to play your instruments while singing songs together, than when you were playing by yourself? How was it different?

- You each contributed your own timbres to the band. Do you think the band would have sounded exactly the same without your instrument?

Discoveries to Make

- Playing instruments together, while singing songs, feels different from playing by ourselves. (Some may prefer group playing, some playing on their own.)

- Each of the children's instruments was an important part of the band's sound.

USING HANDMADE INSTRUMENTS TO ACCOMPANY A STORY

Now children are taking their knowledge of acoustics, timbre, loudness, tempo, and pitch to another level—creating a musical accompaniment to a story as a group. Children will be challenged to think of appropriate ways to use sound to represent characters, actions, and feelings. They'll need to cooperate with others to find solutions to musical and scientific problems, in the dramatic and fun context of a story.

What You'll Need

Picture book with lots of characters and actions

Some suggestions: *One Duck Stuck* by Phyllis Root

Way Up High in a Tall Green Tree by Jan Peck

The Terrible Plop by Ursula Dubosarsky

Just a Little Bit by Ann Tompert

Each child may choose one of his handmade instruments to use in this activity.

Activity to Try

1. This is a two-day activity. On the first day, read the story to your class. Introduce the story by asking them to think about how they could use the sounds of their instruments to accompany the story when you read it again tomorrow.

2. On the second day, go through the story, pausing to ask questions such as these:

   - "Which of the instruments could create a sound like a bear walking? Would it be a loud or soft sound? Slow or fast?"

   - "Is a monkey's voice high-pitched or low-pitched? Can any of our instruments make a high-pitched sound?"

   - "When the duck flies away, how does she feel? How could we show that with the way we play our instruments?"

3. About halfway through your review of the story, stop asking these questions—simply pause and say "Hmm." Let the children take over the thinking and planning process.

4. After the review, have the children decide on the sounds they'll use, and read the story with their musical accompaniment.

Questions to Ask

- Which sounds did you think fit in really well?
- Looking back, are there any sounds you would have changed, or added? (They may decide they'd like a "do-over," which is fine.)
- How did you decide which instruments to use and when to play them?
- What kind of things did you think about when you were deciding?

Discoveries to Make

- Children can add texture, drama, and humor to a story by adding musical sounds to represent characters, actions, and feelings.
- Children can plan musical accompaniments by considering different timbres, pitches, tempos, and degrees of loudness.
- Children can analyze and assess their work.

KEEP THE LEARNING GOING!

Think of the stories that your students love to hear over and over—the ones that especially enchant or amuse them. These stories are good candidates for "soundtrack" projects like this one, using real and nontraditional instruments, singing, and body sounds. It's an engaging, effective way to keep their knowledge of the science of music alive and growing.

GOING FORWARD

The activities in this book are fun and effective learning experiences on their own. Hopefully, though, they'll serve as a springboard for further exploration. Here are some ways to build on these activities to encourage more scientific inquiry.

- Relate the crosscutting concepts to activities in other domains. Examples:
  - Structure and function: When children are building with blocks, ask them if they could build with eggs. Why not?
  - Scale, proportion and quantity: If you're making a salad that requires one cup of grapes, ask the children how many cups you'd need to make three salads.
  - Patterns: Talk about the patterns of the seasons, days of the week, and so on.
  - Energy and matter: What happens to snow when it melts?
- Be open to all questions and help the children find answers for themselves, if possible.
- Call attention to sounds on recordings and in everyday life—"Do you think that sound is a stringed instrument?" "I hear footsteps on the stairs. Do you think it's a child, or an adult? How can you tell?"
- Wonder aloud about things you're curious about. Talk about how you're learning new things, whether by observation or by looking up information. Show children that curiosity and learning are exciting parts of life at any age!

Anderson, Philip W. 1995. "Through the Glass Lightly." *Science 267(5204): 1615.*

Bosse, Sherri, Gera Jacobs, and Tara Lynn Anderson. 2009. "Science in the Air." *Young Children* 64(6): 10–15.

Byrne, David. 2013. *How Music Works.* Edinburgh: Canongate Books.

Cardio Research Web Project. 2016. "Heart Facts on Animals (. . . and Humans)." Cardio Research Web Project, accessed May 7, 2017. http://www.cardio-research.com/quick-facts/animals

Carraher, David W., Mara V. Martinez, and Analucia D. Schliemann. 2008. "Early Algebra and Mathematical Generalization." *ZDM Mathematics Education* 40: 3–22. http://ase.tufts.edu/education/earlyalgebra/publications/2008/mathGeneralization.pdf

Cherny-Scanlon, Xenya. 2014. "Seven Fabrics Inspired by Nature: From the Lotus Leaf to Butterflies and Sharks." The *Guardian,* September 24, 2016. https://www.theguardian.com/sustainable-business/sustainable-fashion-blog/nature-fabrics-fashion-industry-biomimicry

Cornell Lab of Ornithology. 2016. "All About Birds." https://www.allaboutbirds.org/guide/search

Duschl, Richard A., Heidi A.Schweingruber, and Andrew W. Shouse, eds. 2007. *Taking Science to School: Learning and Teaching Science in Grades K–8.* Washington, DC: National Academies Press.

Gopnik, Alison. 2012. "Scientific Thinking in Young Children: Theoretical Advances, Empirical Research, and Policy Implications." *Science* 337 (6102): 1623–1627.

Gopnik, Alison, Andrew N. Meltzoff, and Patricia K. Kuhl. 1999. *The Scientist in the Crib.* New York: William Morrow and Co.

"Irish Folk Spoon Playing." YouTube video, 2:19. Posted by music 21612, July 1, 2012, https://www.youtube.com/watch?v=8SY6JLwdz5c

"Machine with 23 Scraps of Paper–Arthur Ganson." YouTube video, 1:13. Posted by Arthur Ganson, November 25, 2008, https://www.youtube.com/watch?v=PGHonvREHVU

Marigliano, Michelle M., and Michele J. Russo. 2011. "Foster Preschoolers' Critical Thinking and Problem Solving Through Movement." *Young Children* 66 (5): 44–49.

Mullender-Wijnsma, Marijke J., Esther Hartman, Johannes W. de Greeff, Roel J. Bosker, Simone Doolaard, and Chris Visscher. 2015. "Improving Academic Performance of School-age Children by Physical Activity in the Classroom: 1-year Program Evaluation." *Journal of School Health* 85 (6): 365–371.

National Research Council (NRC). 2007. *Taking Science to School: Learning and Teaching Science in Grades K–8.* Washington, DC: National Academies Press.

National Science Teachers Association (NSTA). 2014. "Crosscutting Concepts." http://ngss.nsta.org/CrosscuttingConceptsFull.aspx

National Science Teachers Association (NSTA). 2013. "*NSTA Position Statement: Early Childhood Science Education.*" http://www.nsta.org/about/positions/earlychildhood.aspx

Remedios, R., Nikos K. Logothetis, and Christoph Kayser. 2009. "Monkey Drumming Reveals Common Networks for Perceiving Vocal and Non-vocal Communication Sounds." Proceedings of the

National Academy of Sciences of the United States of America 106(42): 18010-18015.

St. Marie, Terry. 2016. "Play It Again, Sam: The Science of Repeating Things Repeatedly." Terrystarbucker.com. http://www.terrystarbucker.com/2010/10/17/play-it-again-sam-the-science-of-repeating-things-repeatedly/

Texas A&M University. 2007. "How Singing Bats Communicate." ScienceDaily.com. www.sciencedaily.com/releases/2007/10/071018123525.htm

Tierney, Adam and Nina Kraus. 2013. "The Ability to Move to a Beat is Linked to the Consistency of Neural Responses to Sound." *The Journal of Neuroscience* 331(38): 14981-14988.

University of Amsterdam. 2016. "Brain Picks Up the Beat of Music Automatically." ScienceDailycom. www.sciencedaily.com/releases/2016/05/160526125017.htm

Van Enk, John. 2012. "Being Wrong is an Opportunity to Learn." https://spin.atomicobject.com/2012/05/31/being-wrong/

Wilson, Ruth. 2008. "Promoting the Development of Scientific Thinking." Earlychildhoodnews.com. http://www.earlychildhoodnews.com/earlychildhood/article_view.aspx?ArticleId=409

SUGGESTED RECORDINGS OF INSTRUMENTAL MUSIC

Classical:

"Clair de Lune" by Claude Debussy

Clarinet Concerto in A by Mozart, the first few minutes of the first movement

"March" from *The Nutcracker Suite* by Tchaikovsky

"Pine Apple Rag" by Scott Joplin

"Pizzicato" from the ballet *Sylvia* by Leo Delibes

"Radetzky March" by Johann Strauss, Sr.

"The Skater's Waltz" by Émile Waldteufel

Folk/Bluegrass:

"Missing Vassar" by Ricky Skaggs and Kentucky Thunder

"Mulvihill's/Irish Washerwoman" by Séan Tyrrell

"Reels Medley: Blacksmith's Anvil, Bucks of Oranmore, Crosses of Annagh" by Shaskeen

"Shenandoah Valley Breakdown" by Alan Munde

World Music:

"African Djembe Drums" by various artists, from "Experience African Music: African Drumming, African Soukouss Music and West African Dance Music"

"Cumbamba" performed by Jose Conde

"Eastern Journey" by The Biddu Orchestra—This one has a Bollywood flavor.

"Ghana' E" by Willie Colon—This isn't instrumental, but it's very fun dance music that children really like.

"Steel Congo" by Louie Vega

"Sunset Ceremony" by David and Steve Gordon

"Tribal Jungle Music—Fountain of Youth" by Derek and Brandon Fiechter

"West African Soukous" by All Star African Drum Ensemble

Contemporary:

"A Fifth of Beethoven" by Walter Murphy

"Celebration" by Kool & the Gang

"Music Box Dancer" by Frank Mills

INDEX

G

Glockenspiels, viii–ix, 77, 139, 143–145, 149–150

Gross-motor skills, 39–41, 50–51, 55–56, 58–59, 74–75, 86–87, 98, 105–106, 113–119, 129–130, 134–137, 150–153, 165–167

Guitars, 27–28, 49–50, 141–143

H

Hypotheses. *See* Predicting

L

Language skills, 12, 18–19

Listening skills, ix, 11–12, 14–15, 24–28, 31–32, 38–39, 43–45, 52–55, 62, 66–67, 70–71, 82–85, 88–89, 102–104, 109–110, 118–119, 122–123, 157–158, 163–165, 187

Loudness, x–xi, 7–8, 31–37, 52–53, 60–61, 63–64, 66–67, 91–119, 158–159, 169–170, 182–185

M

Mallets, 24, 26, 46, 75, 77–79, 143–146, 149–150, 162, 170–171

Math skills, 12, 99–100

Memory skills, 17–19, 35–36, 38–39, 76

Metal spoons, 46, 58–59, 70–71, 148, 170–171

Metals, 56–64, 66–67, 70–71, 86–87, 145–147, 175

Modeling, 56, 89, 95, 160–161

Musical instruments, viii, 63, 72–73, 84–85

      creating, 175–185

O

Observation skills, ix, 26–28, 47–49, 50–51, 58–59, 63–64, 70–71, 79–81, 163–165, 187

One-to-one correspondence, 128–129

Ordering, 153–155

Outdoor activities, 40–41, 105–106, 150, 157–173, 182

P

Patterns, ix, 3, 12, 29–30, 161, 167–168, 179–180, 187

Pitch, ix–x, 139–155, 161, 163–165, 175–178, 184–185

Plastics, 56, 58–61, 68–71, 75–77, 82–83, 88–89, 147, 175

W

X